Interactive Poetry 11–14

David Kitchen | Imelda Pilgrim

Consultant Michael Jones

www.heinemann.co.uk
✓ Free online support
✓ Useful weblinks
✓ 24 hour online ordering

01865 888058

Heinemann
Inspiring generations

Contents

Introduction to Interactive Poetry 11–14

What is Interactive Poetry 11–14?

Interactive Poetry 11–14 provides unique access to poetry for students aged 11–14. It comprises an integrated Student Book, Software and Teacher's Guide.

How is the Student Book structured?

The Student Book is divided into three main sections (A, B and C) – which notionally reflect Years 7, 8 and 9. However, the poems and activities can be used with any year group to suit individual teaching and learning needs.

Within each main section the student book is divided into:

- Poets
- Theme
- Poem pairings

In each 'Poet' section there are three poems by a poet. In each 'Theme' section there are three poems on a theme. In the 'Poem pairings' section there is one poem pairing in Section A and two in Sections B and C.

How are the teaching and learning organised?

Section introduction: each section opens with an introduction or piece of information relating to the section.

Your learning: for each poem or poem pairing there is a paragraph that explains to the students the skill(s) they are about to learn.

Check your learning: at the end of each learning unit is a section that enables students to reflect on their learning and identify areas of progress or weakness.

Learning extra: an extension activity that enables students to take their learning further, either in lesson time or as homework.

What skills and Framework Objective opportunities are there?

The Student Book offers thorough coverage of the skills students need in order to read and write about poetry. Progression is included within the major sections (A, B and C), as well as within the 'Poets', 'Themes' and 'Poem pairings' sections. Full charts detailing skills coverage and Framework Objective opportunities are on pages 118–21.

What else is available as part of *Interactive Poetry 11–14*?

The ***Interactive Poetry 11–14*** software, comprising three CD-ROMs and accompanying Teacher's Guide, is fully integrated with the Student Book. Resources include:

- all the poems that are in the Student Book, in both text and audio form
- whole-class interactive activities on all of the poems, including linking activities
- images, audio information and video footage that help bring the poems to life
- a Teacher's Guide that provides information and support to deliver the prepared activities
- Easiteach software tools to create customised presentation slides and activities.

Introduction to poetry – an activity for students

Complete the tasks below to find out more about your experiences of poetry.

1. In pairs, ask each other the following questions. Keep a record of the answers.

    a How many poems have you read?
    b Have you enjoyed reading them?
    c Do you have a favourite poem?
    d Can you repeat any lines that you remember from a poem?
    e What kinds of poems do you like most? Can you give an example?
    f What kinds of poems do you like least? Can you give an example?
    g Have you written any poems?
    h Were they good?
    i Can you repeat any lines that you remember from a poem you have written?
    j Why do you think you read poems in your English lessons?

2. Use your answers to the questions to help you put together a few sentences that sum up your partner's attitude to poetry. You can write these or prepare to say them aloud.

3. Join another pair. Take turns to describe your partner's attitude to poetry. Give each partner the chance to say whether the description is accurate or not.

4. As a group, spend more time thinking about the last question: Why do you think you read poems in your English lessons?

    Aim to give at least four reasons that answer this question.

5. Make a group presentation to the class. You could use the following headings to help you organise your ideas:
    - Things we like about poetry
    - Favourite poems
    - Things we don't like about poetry
    - Least-liked poems
    - Our own poems
    - Reasons for reading poems

By now, you and the rest of your class should have a good idea of your different experiences of poetry and your feelings about it. You are about to start reading and studying some more poetry. The writers of this book have chosen these poems carefully, hoping that you will enjoy reading them and that you will learn more about the skills involved in writing poetry. There are funny poems and sad ones, poems that will make you think and poems that will make you want to write poems of your own. Read on. We hope we have chosen well!

Norman Silver was born in Cape Town, South Africa, and has lived in England since 1969. He's keen on computers and used to work with young people who were in trouble with the police. In this section you will look at three of his poems.

Electronic Brain

Norman Silver

Your learning

Poems can be structured to make you feel you are waiting for something to happen – that is often part of the fun. Here you will look at the effects of repetition, the ending and of making a machine the 'voice' of the poem.

Electronic Brain

I am an intelligent machine:
I read *Computer Weekly* magazine.
    My ancestors were robotic,
    their procedures idiotic –
with not much going on behind the screen. 5

I am an intelligent machine:
everything I say I really mean.
    My dictionary's extensive,
    my grammar's comprehensive,
I'm never flummoxed by the unforeseen. 10

I am an intelligent machine:
my program lets me vary my routine.
    I think it's prejudicial
    to call me artificial –
I can tell you who I am and where I've been. 15

I am an intelligent machine:
my processors are bug-free and serene.
    I have friendly interfaces,
    gigantic databases ...
Oops! FATAL ERROR: MEMORY WIPED CLEAN. 20

EXPLANATIONS

ancestors people from whom you are descended, such as great-grandparents

extensive very large

comprehensive covering almost everything

flummoxed confused

prejudicial biased, unfair

serene calm

interfaces connections between computer users

1. Pick out the words/phrases in the first stanza that show that this modern computer does not think much of earlier models.

2. From time to time, writers give human characteristics to something that is not human. This is known as personification. Probably the most common example of this in literature is talking animals. In this poem, it is the computer that speaks like a human being.

   Choose three phrases that give the impression that the computer is overconfident or big-headed. Explain why you chose them.

   Here is an example:
   The computer says it is 'never flummoxed by the unforeseen'.
   The message here is that it can cope with anything.
   The emphasis should probably be on the word 'never', which suggests that the computer is completely reliable.

3. Personification can change the way an object or a creature is seen in a poem. Some people would say that it makes the thing more 'solid' or 'understandable'. It can certainly affect our feelings about what is being described. Finish these sentences:
   - The best thing about the computer being the 'voice' of the poem is...
   - It gives you the impression that...

4. When people repeat words, it is usually to draw attention to them. Poetry is no different from speech in this respect, but in a poem repetition is usually done with great care and for a specific reason.
   What words are repeated in every stanza of this poem?
   What is the effect of these words coming up again and again?

5. Re-read the last line of the poem. What is the effect of putting the final words in capital letters? Discuss what it means and how far you think it changes the effect of the whole poem.

Information

Stanza
A group of lines that go together in a poem, also called a verse. 'Electronic Brain' has four stanzas.

Check your learning

a Give two reasons why a writer might structure their work to put the emphasis on the ending.
b Suggest two other examples from your reading or from television and film where you have seen this work well.
c What have you learnt about personification?
Share your answers with each other.

Learning extra

Write a short piece in the voice of a modern mobile phone.

a Think about all the advantages of new mobile phones.
b Let your phone be as big-headed as the computer.
c Have a twist in your final sentence.

I Want Trainers

NORMAN SILVER

Your learning

The 'speaker' in a poem is not always the poet. Here you will explore the difference between a poem's creator and a poem's 'voice'.

I Want Trainers

I want trainers
that stand out in a crowd,
that mark you number one on the block,
that raise you off the concrete,
5 that stamp your identity on the streets,
that make your every footstep a dance,
that find their own way through town,
that magnetize the eyes of your mates,

with innersoles like trampolines,
10 with tongues that reach your knees,
with laces that hang loose,
with gold-plated lettering,
with treads deeper than tractor wheels,
with footprints that spell danger,
15 with hugely inflated price-tags,

because the way I am I'm a nonentity,
because even Sam has got a pair,
because you love me and you're my parents,
because feet need all the attention they can get,
20 because I'm suffering severe shoe envy,
because what I wear is what I am,
because if I don't get them I might as well be DEAD!

EXPLANATIONS

nonentity someone of no importance

1 In groups, listen to each other reading the poem aloud. You could try male/female voices. You could try a strong, positive voice, then a sad, whining voice. Which ones work best and why?

2 The narrator is the person who tells you what is going on.

a Do you think the narrator in this poem is male or female? What is your evidence?

b What age might the narrator of the poem be? Explain why.

3 Narrators in poems often provide detail and opinions. Re-read the poem, then copy and complete the table below, adding your own thoughts.

	Words and phrases from the poem	Your own words and phrases
What trainers do		It makes the person sound important
What they should be like	'with innersoles like trampolines' 'with...	
Why the trainers are needed		The simile suggests...

information

Simile

A picture created in the mind by comparing one thing with another, using the words 'like' or 'as', e.g. 'he had a kick like a mule'.

4 A poem's writer and narrator can be very different. This poem contains clues that the narrator is probably a young person. See if you can find three clues and explain why you chose them. Here is an example:

'because if I don't get them I might as well be DEAD.' I chose this because a young person would say this, but obviously wouldn't mean it!

5 Put the following statements in order, with the one that describes the poem most effectively first.

- The poem shows how important trainers are.
- The poem shows how expensive trainers can be.
- The poem shows how young people think too much of trainers.
- The poem shows how parents don't take trainers seriously.

Explain how you made your choice.

Check your learning

Use what you have learnt through this poem to complete these sentences:

- The narrator gives you the impression that ...
- The main effect of the poem is ...

Share your completed answers with each other.

Learning extra

The second stanza is full of exaggeration. Write your own exaggerated descriptions. Here are three subjects to get you started:

- the amount of homework you get
- the size of your house
- the loudness of someone's voice.

Life is a Ball

NORMAN SILVER

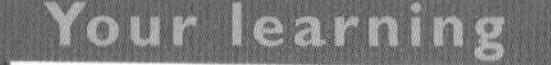

Some poems offer you the chance to understand a subject by comparing one thing with another. Here you will look at how an extended comparison works.

Life is a Ball

Nobody loves me,
no one at all.
To them it's a game
with me as the ball.

They kick me around
from one post to the other.
You know who I mean –
the old man and my mother.

I've tried to complain
but the linesman's blind.
He won't flag offside
when they're unkind.

Nobody cares
the way that I'm booted.
I've asked to be mended
or substituted.

But the crowd shouts:
Why are we waiting?
The coach doesn't bother
that my air's deflating.

Whether fair or foul
the game continues,
till my leather's worn
to its bare sinews.

EXPLANATIONS

deflating losing air, becoming flat

substituted taken off during a match

old man slang for father

worn to its bare sinews worn down so it's in a poor condition

1 Look at the following four reactions to the poem. Which response gets the sense of the poem best? Rank the responses in order, where 1 is the most effective and 4 is the least effective.

a *It's like the adults give out rules but then they ignore them.*
b *A football gets kicked around and some kids get passed from one person to another, especially when grown-ups are busy.*
c *You can picture somebody who gets no support from anyone.*
d *It's good because adults are always saying things that make children feel deflated.*

Discuss your own initial reactions to the poem.

2 The narrator compares living to being a football. Describing one thing as another like this is called metaphor. When it runs right through a poem or piece of writing it is called an extended metaphor. This is often used to build up a strong and coherent picture of a character or situation.

Discuss with a partner who or what the people or things in the list below could be in the poem. The first one has been done as an example, to show you what to do.

football	me, everyone, young people *Is the football a picture of one person or all people, or of young people in particular?*
footballers	adults, mother, father, parents
crowd	friends, family, all the other adults, everyone
inesman	judge, policeman, teacher, social worker
coach	older brother/sister, PE teacher, head teacher, form teacher
offside	unfair punishment, being hit, sarcasm, being cheated

3 Write two paragraphs describing your responses to this poem. Try to express how you feel about the person described and his/her situation. You should include:

- your personal response to the poem
- whether the poem is a serious or light-hearted look at life (or both)
- what the effect is of using the extended metaphor of the football.

Check your learning

Complete these sentences:

- The image of life as a football game works/doesn't work because …
- The part of the extended metaphor that I like best is …

Compare your answers with a partner's.

Learning extra

Try comparing your own life to a week in school. You could start like this:

- Life is a timetable …
- Nobody tells me where I'm supposed to be, then they moan when I'm not there …
- My …

Linking the Norman Silver poems

Your learning

Poets engage a reader's attention and interest in a range of ways. Here you will look at how Norman Silver's poems relate to your own experiences and how he captures this in his choice of subject matter.

1 Look again at all three poems by Norman Silver. What is the one thing in each poem that you are most likely to remember? This could be a detail, an idea or the overall feeling that you get from the poem.

2 You are going to write your own report on Norman Silver's poem.

a Make a copy of the table on page 11. Make sure you allow plenty of space to write down what you and a partner have to say. Do not copy the examples that are shown in some of the boxes.

b Fill in the three boxes yourself for each poem. If you are not sure how to start, look at the examples in the table of how one student started her answer on 'Life is a Ball'.

c Ask your partner to tell you what s/he thinks.

d When you have made a note of each other's answers, talk about the differences in your responses. What do you learn from each other?

3 **a** What would you ask Norman Silver if you met him? Look at the description of him at the start of this section on page 4, at his poems and at the responses you wrote for question 2. Decide on three questions you would like to ask him.

b You are going to put someone in the 'hot seat' as Norman Silver and ask that person your questions. If you are in the hot seat, use what you have discovered about the poet from this section of the book to help you provide convincing answers. If you are listening, be ready to say whether the answers fit in with the impression created by the poems.

4 Write a paragraph about the impression that Norman Silver's poems have made on you. Use what you have learnt from your work on questions 1, 2 and 3. You could look in particular at:

- his understanding of people's worries
- his concern for those who have a difficult time
- his realism
- his sense of humour.

If you are not sure where to begin, you could start by completing some of the following sentences.

- One striking thing about Norman Silver's poetry is…
- This is captured well in…
- Young people will easily relate to…
- In ……… there is a strong sense of…
- My own favourite line…

The Norman Silver Poem Report

	What the poem is about	How the poem relates to our experience	The line(s) that capture this best
Life is a Ball	It's about life as a sort of human football. ………………………	It's interesting because some young people do get a bad deal and it's not just from adults. …………………………	'Nobody cares/the way that I'm booted.' ……………………
Electronic Brain	………………………	………………………	………………………
I Want Trainers	………………………	………………………	………………………

Check your learning

Complete these three sentences:

- I thought that the poems related to our experience in …
- When I heard my partner's answers, I …
- Norman Silver's choice of words is often …

Share your completed answers.

Learning extra

Prepare a book cover for a collection of Norman Silver's poems that includes the three you have studied here. Choose a title and plan a design for the cover. Write the blurb that will go on the back in order to attract readers to take a further look.

John Agard was born in Guyana in 1949 and worked there as a journalist. He moved to Britain in 1977 and became a touring lecturer on Caribbean culture. As a result, he has visited over 2000 schools and is now well known both as a writer and a performer.

The Soldiers Came

John Agard

Your learning

Poets find different ways to share their thoughts, feelings and messages. Here you will identify what the main ideas of the poem are and see how they are developed and structured.

The Soldiers Came

The soldiers came
and dropped their bombs.
The soldiers didn't take long
to bring the forest down.

5 With the forest gone
the birds are gone.
With the birds gone
who will sing their song?

But the soldiers forgot
10 to take the forest
out of the people's hearts.
The soldiers forgot
to take the birds
out of the people's dreams.
15 And in the people's dreams
the birds still sing their song.

Now the children
are planting seedlings
to help the forest grow again.
20 They eat a simple meal of soft rice
wrapped in banana leaf.
And the land welcomes their smiling
like a shower of rain.

1 John Agard has divided his poem into four stanzas.

a Decide on a short description for each stanza. For the first stanza you could choose from the following:

- The arrival of the soldiers
- The dropping of the bombs
- Soldiers bomb the forest.

b The third and fourth stanzas are longer than the first two. Why do you think the poet has done this? Think especially about:

- what happens in them
- what that tells you about life in the forest.

2 Look at the lines in the poem that describe what the soldiers did.

a Discuss your reactions to what the soldiers did. Look particularly at the verbs *came, didn't take long, forgot.*

b How would you describe the soldiers in your own words?

c What message does the poet convey about the soldiers' behaviour?

3 Look at what the poem says about the children; look at how the poem ends. Which of the following best describes the main message of this poem? Why?

It's about the belief that ...
... peace is stronger than war.
... ordinary people can overcome what soldiers do.
... those who try to destroy things do not win.
... powerful people never think of the damage they cause.
... you can put right even the most terrible situations.

4 Write at least two paragraphs explaining how the poem is structured and develops.

You could look at:

- the impression given by each of the four stanzas
- the contrast between the soldiers and the people/children who live in the forest
- the difference between the start and the end of the poem
- the overall message of the poem and how this affects the reader.

Check your learning

Complete these two sentences.

- The way this poem changes across the four stanzas has shown me ...
- The contrast between different parts of the poem helps to ...

Compare your answers with a partner's; talk about how far you agree about the way you see this poem.

Learning extra

Write your own piece about bullies; challenge their power just as this poem challenges the power of soldiers. Include the words that John Agard uses:

Bullies ... came ... didn't take long ... forgot

What The Teacher Said When Asked: What Er We Avin For Geography Miss?

John Agard

Your learning

Poetry is sometimes about what people dream might happen. As you explore the way words are used here, you will learn about using quotations in your responses to a poem.

What The Teacher Said When Asked: What Er We Avin For Geography Miss?

This morning I've got too much energy
much too much for geography

I'm in a high mood
so class don't think me crude
5 but you can stuff latitude and longitude

I've had enough of the earth's crust
today I want to touch the clouds

Today I want to sing out loud
and tear all maps to shreds

10 I'm not settling for river beds
I want the sky and nothing less

Today I couldn't care if east turns west
Today I've got so much energy
I could do press-ups on the desk
15 but that won't take much out of me

Today I'll dance on the globe
in a rainbow robe

While you class remain seated
on your natural zone
20 with your pens and things
watching my contours grow wings

All right class, see you later.
If the headmaster asks for me
say I'm a million dreaming degrees
25 beyond the equator

a million dreaming degrees
beyond the equator.

EXPLANATIONS

latitude imaginary lines parallel to the Equator for the purpose of locating places

longitude imaginary lines from pole to pole for the purpose of locating places

1 What words/phrases of your own would you use to describe this teacher? List at least two words and two phrases.

2 When you are quoting less than a line of a poem, you simply put the words in inverted commas in your sentence. Here is one example:

In this poem, the teacher is unusual. Instead of being tired,
she says she has 'too much energy' to stay in the classroom.

a Now read lines 5–7 and complete this sentence:

- Instead of being depressed, this teacher is 'in a ...' and clearly does not want to ...

b Read lines 8–11. Use the phrase 'tear all maps to shreds' in a sentence that explains how the teacher sounds fed up with geography. Include the quotation in your explanation and remember to place inverted commas around it.

3 When you quote a complete line or more from a poem, you normally set out the lines as they appear in the poem. You still need to use inverted commas, as in the example below.

The teacher seems to be tired of geography and ready for a change:
'I'm not settling for river beds
I want the sky and nothing less'.
Wanting the sky sounds more like a dream than a real alternative.

Read the lines below, then write a sentence commenting on how much energy this geography teacher has. Then write a sentence about the humour and/or the exaggeration.

'Today I've got so much energy
I could do press-ups on the desk'.

4 Write a paragraph or two about the picture the poem gives you of this geography teacher. Use quotations in the ways you have practised in questions 2 and 3. Remember that:

- quotations are the evidence for the point you are making about the poem
- quotations have inverted commas around them
- if you quote a line or more, you need to set it out as it appears in the poem.

Check your learning

Work in pairs; explain to each other how you use quotations in writing about a poem. Ask each other questions to make sure you are both clear about what to do when using quotations.

Learning extra

Imagine you are in this geography class and the deputy head finds you without a teacher. You are chosen to go and tell the head what has happened. What will you say?

Checking Out Me History

JOHN AGARD

Your learning

Some poems are a manifesto, a statement in which the poet believes passionately. Here you will explore how John Agard expresses his feelings about how history can often be presented. You will also practise using quotations.

EXPLANATIONS

Nanny de maroon (1700–40) fearless female freedom fighter from Jamaica

Shaka (1785–1828) Zulu leader

Caribs/Arawaks the people who lived in the Caribbean before Europeans arrived there

Mary Seacole (1805–81) pioneering Jamaican nurse

Checking Out Me History

Dem tell me
Dem tell me
Wha dem want to tell me

Bandage up me eye with me own history
5 Blind me to me own identity

Dem tell me bout 1066 and all dat
dem tell me bout Dick Whittington and he cat
But Toussaint L'Ouverture
no dem never tell me bout dat

10 Toussaint
a slave
with vision
lick back
Napoleon
15 battalion
and first Black
Republic born
Toussaint de thorn
to de French
20 Toussaint de beacon
of de Haitian Revolution

Dem tell me bout de man who discover de balloon
and de cow who jump over de moon
Dem tell me bout de dish run away with de spoon
25 but dem never tell me bout Nanny de maroon

Nanny
See-far woman
of mountain dream
fire-woman struggle
30 hopeful stream
to freedom river

Dem tell me bout Lord Nelson and Waterloo
but dem never tell me bout Shaka de great Zulu
Dem tell me bout Columbus and 1492
35 but what happen to de Caribs and de Arawaks too

Dem tell me bout Florence Nightingale and she lamp
and how Robin Hood used to camp
Dem tell me bout ole King Cole was a merry ole soul
but dem never tell me bout Mary Seacole

40 From Jamaica
she travel far
to the Crimean War
she volunteer to go
and even when de British said no
45 she still brave the Russian snow
a healing star
among the wounded
a yellow sunrise
to the dying

50 Dem tell me
Dem tell me wha dem want to tell me
But now I checking out me own history
I carving out me identity

1. What is your first impression of what John Agard is saying in this poem?

2. Look at statements a–e below. Decide which parts of the poem they could be connected with. List the lines you choose. The first one has been done for you.

   a They use history to hide things – *lines 4–5*
   b She was a woman with vision and imagination
   c They tell you all sorts of nursery rhyme nonsense and they miss out the important things
   d She wouldn't take 'no' for an answer
   e You only get told what other people want to tell you

3. Toussaint L'Ouverture (1743–1803) was a black slave. He led the people of Haiti to independence against Spanish, British and French troops. When John Agard writes about how he admires him, he doesn't merely say that he beat Napoleon, but that he 'lick back' Napoleon. This gives a sense that he swept the great leader out of his way.

   Look at John Agard's descriptions of Nanny de maroon (lines 27–31) and Mary Seacole (lines 46–9).

   a Quote the words that give you the sense that these women are more than a good fighter and a good nurse.
   b What impression do the words you have chosen give you of these two people?

   If you are not sure how to set out your quotations, look back at question 3 on page 15.

4. Write a paragraph about how John Agard expresses his passion for black history and its heroes. Use quotations to support what you say.

   You might look at:

   - how other people, according to the poem, seem to use history
   - the poet's descriptions of black heroes from history
   - how the poem ends.

Check your learning

Share with a partner your answers to questions 3 and 4.
Did you make good use of quotations?
Did you capture a sense of how the poet used this poem to say what he felt?
How could you make your answers clearer?

Learning extra

List five people who you think deserve to be remembered in history; they can be living or dead, famous or unknown. Write a description of one of them, showing what is or was special about them. Try to use a powerful image (John Agard uses 'stream' and 'sunrise').

Linking the John Agard poems

Your learning

Here, you will be looking back at the three poems by John Agard. You will explore what connects them and what makes each of them distinctive.

1. Look back at the three poems by John Agard. Choose one of the following words to describe each poem:

- angry
- weary
- light-hearted
- uncertain
- puzzled
- factual.

2. John Agard's poems often turn things upside down. As a result, he makes his readers look at things in a new way, or challenge their own assumptions. Connect each of the statements below with one or more of the poems. Copy out the statements and write the most appropriate poem title next to each one.

- *The main character in the poem behaves in an unexpected way.*
- *It finishes by going back to the point where it started.*
- *Things are very different at the end of the poem from the way they were at the start.*
- *It's about how things ought to be.*
- *It uses a series of examples.*
- *It's about having dreams.*
- *It's about wanting to do something different.*

information

Simile
A picture created in the mind by comparing one thing with another, using the words 'like' or 'as', e.g. 'He had a face like a thundercloud.'

3. Choose your favourite two or three lines from each poem. Write them out and explain why you chose them, for example:

In 'The Soldiers Came', I chose the simile:
'And the land welcomes their smiling
Like a shower of rain.'
I like the idea that their smiles are refreshing the world just like a shower makes everything look new and sparkling when the sun comes out again.

4. Choose the poem that you think is the most unusual of the three. Write four sentences about it, using these sentence starters.

- The poem that I felt to be unusual was …
- What made it different was …
- I particularly liked the way …
- The phrase that really stuck in my mind was …

5. Like many poets, Agard encourages his readers to take a second look at aspects of the world. In these poems he suggests that:
   - soldiers don't have all the power after all
   - teachers might sometimes want more than a classroom
   - history needs to be written with a lot more people included.

   Talk in pairs about how far these poems have encouraged you to think again about any of the subjects. Are you more won over by a humorous poem or a serious one? Which poem is most effective in your eyes? Why? In your discussion, you could comment on some or all of the following:
   - language
   - mood
   - structure
   - ideas.

   Remember to talk about all three poems, not just the one you think is most effective.

6. Choose two of the poems by John Agard that you have been studying.

   a Write at least two paragraphs, picking out what you think is effective in each poem. Remember to use quotations to support what you say.

   b Next, write about the ways in which the poems are different.

   c Finally, write down which one you prefer and why.

Check your learning

Write down what you have learnt about:
- the differences between the poems
- what makes each poem stand out
- what links the poems together.

Share your answers with a partner and together choose the most important point you think you have made.

Learning extra

'What The Teacher Said…' starts with the line: 'This morning I've got too much energy'. Take that as a starting point for a poem or story of your own where you turn your normal day upside down. Have fun and dream big!

Elizabeth Jennings worked as a librarian and was a keen filmgoer. Her pet hatred was vagueness. She became a major poet because of her sharp mind and different ways of looking at the world around her.

The Moth's Plea

ELIZABETH JENNINGS

Your learning

Poets are able to create the mood of a poem in many ways. Here you will look at the choice of words as well as the use of alliteration and personification to help you comment on the impression they make.

The Moth's Plea

I am a disappointment
And much worse.
You hear a flutter, you expect a brilliance of wings,
Colours dancing, a bright
5 Flutter, but then you see
A brown, bedraggled creature
With a shamefaced, unclean look
Darting upon your curtains and clothes,
Fighting against the light.
10 I hate myself. It's no wonder you hate me.

I meddle among your things,
I make a meal out of almost any cloth,
I hide in cupboards and scare
Any who catch me unaware.
15 I am your enemy – the moth.

You try to keep me away
But I'm wily and when I do
Manage to hide, you chase me, beat me, put
Horrible-smelling balls to poison me.
20 Have you ever thought what it's like to be
A parasite,
Someone who gives you a fright,
Who envies the rainbow colours of the bright
Butterflies who hover round all day?

25 O please believe that I do understand how it feels
To be awake in and be afraid of the night.

EXPLANATIONS

bedraggled very untidy, messed up
shamefaced showing embarrassment or shame
meddle interfere
wily cunning, crafty
parasite someone who lives at someone else's expense

1. What is your first impression of the moth in this poem? Which words give you that impression?

2. In the first stanza, the moth describes itself as a 'disappointment'.
   Using the poem, explain what people expect to see when they hear the sound of wings. What do they actually see? Find words in the poem that support your answers.

3. Discuss how the moth feels about itself. Find three words or phrases to support your point of view. Sum up your impression in a sentence or two of your own.

4. This poem uses alliteration to highlight some phrases. Alliteration is where two or more words that are close together start with the same sound, for example: 'a brown bedraggled creature' (line 6). The alliteration focuses the reader's attention on what the moth looks like. Find another example of alliteration in the poem and say what it highlights.

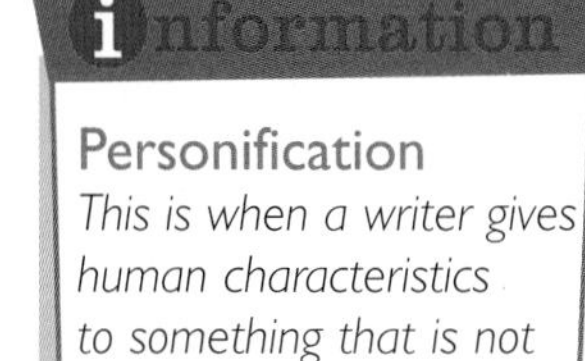

Personification
This is when a writer gives human characteristics to something that is not human.

5. Elizabeth Jennings could have chosen to describe the moth using the third person (he/she/it). Instead, she writes as if the moth itself is speaking to us. What are the effects of choosing to give the moth a voice? Describe your response by completing the sentence below.
   - A description would tell you what the moth looked like but not …

6. Write two or three paragraphs about the impression the poet creates of the moth in this poem. Look at:
   - what happens in each stanza
   - the poet's choice of words
   - the feelings in the poem
   - the difference between butterflies and moths.

Check your learning

What picture of moths do you have in your mind after looking at this poem? Write two or three sentences and share them with a partner. Talk about where you agree and where you think differently. Do the differences matter?

Learning extra

Write a piece of your own about an unloved creature. It could be a spider, mouse, ant, hedgehog, worm, slug, beetle, frog, wasp, sparrow … make your own choice. Start as Elizabeth Jennings does, with 'I am a …'

Casting a Spell

ELIZABETH JENNINGS

Your learning

Poets often write poems that appear to be about more than one thing. Here, you will look at how Elizabeth Jennings does this. Then you will practise writing your own poem.

Casting a Spell

Learn a spell. It takes some time
First you must have the gift of rhyme,
New images, a melody.
Verse will do but poetry
Sometimes will come if you have luck. 5
Play tines, blow trumpets, learn to pluck
The harp. The best of spells are cast
When you have written words to last,
Rich in subtle rhythms and
Right words which most will understand. 10
Casting a spell's a secret skill
Which few learn fast. No act of will
On your part hands the gift to you.
Words must surprise and yet ring true.
False sorcerers are everywhere 15
But the true magic's deep and rare.

EXPLANATIONS

tines musical forks, used as tuned percussion
will effort, determination
sorcerers magicians

1. Discuss what the poem is about from your first reading of it. You might come up with more than one answer!

2. Now take a more careful look. Here's how one pupil explained two lines from the poem:

   'The best of spells are cast
   When you have written words to last'
   I think the poet is saying that what matters is finding something to tell others that is true today and will remain true for the whole of your life.

   Choose two short sections of the poem, maybe a line or two in length. Write explanations of what the poet is saying for someone who finds the poem hard to understand.

3. Throughout the poem, the poet suggests that a lyric is like a spell because:

   a You have to be taught how to do it.
   b It needs a bit of special magic to come alive.
   c You need a bit of good fortune for it to work.
   d The skill required is hidden.

   Find lines in the poem that give evidence for each of these statements.

information

Lyric
A poem expressing personal feelings; the most basic type of lyric is the song.

4. You are going to write a poem about the ingredients for friendship; you will be giving advice just as Elizabeth Jennings does.

   Step 1: Decide what friendship should include. Here are some ideas to get you started:

   - keeping secrets
   - being fair
   - standing up for one another.

   Step 2: Decide what good friends need to be able to do. Think about:

   - what they say
   - their listening skills
   - trust
   - their sense of humour
   - how they tell you difficult things
   - what they're like in a crisis
   - what they buy you.

   Step 3: Write the first draft of your poem; try to use some of the same features that Elizabeth Jennings uses. This could include:

   - writing about the ingredients of friendship
   - treating friendship as a kind of magic
   - offering advice and warnings
   - bringing it all together in one stanza.

Check your learning

In pairs, read each other's poems, then pick the best line or phrase from each other's work. Suggest at least two changes that might improve each poem. Complete the final draft of your poem.

Learning extra

Write about the ingredients of a good poem or a good song. Give examples of the things that you think work well.

The Fish's Warning

ELIZABETH JENNINGS

Your learning

Poems communicate meaning through the choices they make about the words and the lines in their writing. Here you will explore the effects of the words used to describe the fish, and the importance of pauses in poetry.

The Fish's Warning

Stay by the water, stand on your shadow, stare
At my quick gliding, my darting body. You're made of air
And I of water. I do not know if you mean to throw
Your line, I move very fast, swim with fins much quicker
5 Than your thin arms. Rushes will hide me and will
Darken me. I'm a pulse of silver, something the moon
    tossed down.
I am frail for your finding but one whom only the night
    can drown.

EXPLANATIONS

gliding moving smoothly
Rushes plants with thin tall leaves, often found by rivers
frail fragile, weak, easily broken

1. Find as many rhymes as you can in this poem. What is the effect of including these rhymes in the poem?

2. It is natural to pause at the end of a line, but sometimes there is a pause in the middle of a line, for example:

   '... stare
   At my quick gliding, my darting body. You're made of air
   And I of water.'

   Here, the pause after 'my darting body' indicates that the description of the fish has finished. The narrator now moves on to point out the difference between humans and fish.

   A definite pause in the middle of a line is called a caesura. Usually, it is marked by a full stop. Find another place where the poem pauses in the middle of a line; say why you think the author has placed a pause here.

3. The poem's title describes it as a 'warning'. What words or phrases give a sense of warning, menace or threat? How would you sum up the atmosphere the poem creates?

4. The poet builds up a clear picture of the fish. Look at these words and phrases:
   - 'my quick gliding, my darting body'
   - 'a pulse of silver'
   - 'something the moon tossed down'
   - 'frail for your finding'
   - 'swim with fins much quicker/Than your thin arms'

   With a partner, make notes on what each of these descriptions suggests to you, for example: *'pulse' is used in Physics and 'a pulse of silver' makes me think that the fish is almost electric as it darts around.*

5. Write a paragraph or two about the effect of the poem, using the sentence starters below.
   - The first sentence of the poem tells the reader to ...
   - This makes you think that ...
   - The poem contrasts the fish with ...
   - The effect of this is ...
   - The descriptions of the fish create ...
   - The poem gives me an impression of ...

Check your learning

With a partner, check that you both understand what a caesura is, then complete these sentences.

- The way the lines are laid out in a poem matters because ...
- The choice of descriptive words tells you ...

Compare your answers with your partner's.

Learning extra

Write 6–12 lines describing an animal. Try to capture what the animal is like. You could begin: 'I am the follower, tucked into your shadow ...'

Linking the Elizabeth Jennings poems

Your learning

You have looked at three poems by Elizabeth Jennings. Here you will reflect on their similarities and differences and offer a personal response to them.

1. Which poem …

   … makes a contrast between two animals?
   … is about an animal trying to avoid being captured?
   … is about an animal that hates itself?
   … is about the way people say things?
   … starts with instructions?
   … is about an animal that moves quickly?

2. Answer the two questions below and say why you chose the poems you did.

   a Which poem speaks most directly to you, the reader?

   b Which poem creates the strongest feeling of sadness for you?

3. Below are four sentences about the poems, each with three alternative endings. Choose the most appropriate ending for each one and write out the complete sentence. Comment on why you made the choice you did.

   The moth and the fish are both creatures …

   … who feel threatened.
   … for whom we feel sympathy.
   … who have to hide from humans.

   'The Moth's Plea' and 'Casting a Spell' …

   … both deal with surprises.
   … both ask you to think differently.
   … both speak directly to the reader.

   'Casting a Spell' and 'The Fish's Warning' …

   … both give you instructions.
   … both use alliteration.
   … have very different approaches to their subject.

   All three poems …

   … focus clearly on one thing.
   … try to explain something.
   … offer an unusual way of looking at the world.

4 Read the statements below and say whether you think they are true or false. Find evidence to support your opinion and comment on it.

a 'Casting a Spell' is different from the other two poems because it is in the form of instructions rather than description.

b The most mysterious of the three poems is 'The Fish's Warning'.

c You get a sense of how the creature feels in 'The Moth's Plea' that is not there in 'The Fish's Warning'.

d There is a sense of hopelessness in all three poems.

5 Write two or three paragraphs introducing these poems to a new reader of your own age. Point out the links between the poems as well as the ways in which they are distinctive and different. Use quotations to support what you say.

Use your answers to questions 1–4 and what you have learnt from looking at each of the poems individually. You may want to do this by:

- writing a sentence or two about each poem
- pointing out things that are similar in two or more poems
- focusing on what the poems do well
- picking out particular phrases and commenting on their effect
- saying what you think is most striking about these poems.

information

Using quotations

When you are quoting less than a line of a poem, put the words in inverted commas in your sentence. When you are quoting a complete line or more from a poem, you normally set out the lines as they appear in the poem. You still need to use inverted commas. See page 15 for examples.

Check your learning

Work in pairs. Read each other your answers for question 5, and pick one effective and helpful sentence from each piece of writing. Choose one sentence that might be difficult to understand and try to make it clearer.

Learning extra

If you wanted to find out if someone had understood these poems, what would you ask them? Work out ten questions that you could ask to test a reader's understanding.

The English language has nearly half a million words, over one billion people speak it and everyone seems to have an opinion on it. Here, you will look at three different poems about language and extend your own reading and writing skills as a result.

Why English is so Hard

ANON

Your learning

In this poem, some of the strange things about the English language are collected together. Here you will have the chance to look at how rhyme schemes work before writing a poem in rhyme yourself.

Why English is so Hard

We'll begin with a box, and the plural is boxes;
But the plural of ox should be oxen, not oxes.
Then one fowl is a goose, but two are called geese;
Yet the plural of moose should never be meese.
5 You may find a lone mouse or a whole lot of mice,
But the plural of house is houses, not hice.
If the plural of man is always called men,
Why shouldn't the plural of pan be called pen?
The cow in the plural may be cows or kine.
10 But the plural of vow is vows, not vine.
And I speak of a foot, and you show me your feet,
But I give you a boot – would a pair be called beet?
If one is a tooth and a whole set are teeth,
Why shouldn't the plural of booth be called beeth?
15 If the singular is this, and the plural is these,
Should the plural of kiss be nicknamed kese?
Then one may be that, and three may be those,
Yet the plural of hat would never be hose.
We speak of a brother, and also of brethren,
20 But though we say mother, we never say methren.
The masculine pronouns are he, his, and him,
But imagine the feminine she, shis, and shim!
So our English, I think you will all agree,
Is the trickiest language you ever did see.

EXPLANATIONS

vow promise

1. Look back through the poem and find five words that have been made up. Check to make sure that they are not in a dictionary.

2. Words that rhyme may sound alike at their ends, for example 'away' and 'today'. Rhyme schemes in poems show you how words rhyme at the end of lines. Normally each rhyming sound is given a letter alphabetically. In this poem, the rhyme scheme of the first three lines looks like this:

We'll begin with a box, and the plural is boxes;	a
But the plural of ox should be oxen, not oxes.	a
Then one fowl is a goose, but two are called geese;	b

   a What letters would you put at the end of the fourth and fifth lines?

   b Work out the rhyme scheme for the whole poem.

3. This kind of rhyme scheme is called rhyming couplets, because pairs of lines rhyme at their ends. There are also several lines that are linked by rhymes that are not at the end. In this poem, *house* and *mouse* rhyme. Note: it is important to say the words aloud to hear whether the sounds are same.

   a Do *foot* and *boot* rhyme exactly? The answer depends on your accent.

   b Find five more rhymes that appear in the middle of lines in this poem. Remember: you are listening for matching sounds, not matching letters.

4. Now write your own silly rhyming poem. Don't worry too much about meaning, work mainly on the sound of what you are writing. This is often called nonsense verse. Use the box below to help you find words that rhyme. If you can't think how to start, here are three possible first lines:

The spiggy from Rumsfold was two hours late ...

The heligo hippo kept his head on a plate ...

The underarm fishers used sharks' teeth for bait ...

Rhyme box

date	eight	fate	great
grate	gate	hate	late
plate	rate	state	wait
weight	bait	mate	skate
pair	air	stair	
care	bear	spare	
hair	chair	despair	
pear	scare	wear	

Check your learning

In pairs, listen to each other's poems, and choose two good lines from each one. What makes them 'good' – is it the idea, the rhyme, the humour? Now agree on two lines that might be improved. Work together on the choice of words in those lines in order to improve them.

Learning extra

Look at the plurals in the poem. List all the ways of making plurals that you can find, for example, adding s, so *vow* becomes *vows*.

Little Acorns

DAVID HORNER

Your learning

Poets enjoy language. Here you will see what David Horner makes of the language of poetry. You will study some of those words and write a similar poem of your own.

Little Acorns

if the oaks tell jokes
if the yew does a cool haiku
if the elm excels at villanelles
if the ash can bash out a sonnet
5 if the sycamore cares for metaphor
if the weeping-willow trees like similes
if the chestnut's nuts about raps and chants
if the pines and the limes write lines that rhyme
if the hickory's trick is the limerick
10 if the apple counts in syllables
if the firs prefer free verse
if the plum makes puns
THEN
LET
15 THIS
BE MY
POETREE

EXPLANATIONS

villanelles a type of poem that has 19 lines and two end-of-line rhymes

syllable a single sound within a word, e.g. 'hit' has one syllable and 'hitting' has two

yew, elm, ash, sycamore, hickory types of tree

1. Discuss what you immediately notice about this poem.

2. 'Little Acorns' is full of words about poetry. Copy and complete the table below, writing in the correct definition from the list.

metaphor	
haiku	
sonnet	
simile	where a writer compares one thing with another, using 'like' or 'as'
limerick	
pun	
free verse	

- a play on words that have the same sound but different meanings
- a poem with only 17 syllables
- a five-line comic poem
- where the writer writes about something as if it were something else
- poetry that does not use regular rhyme or rhythm
- a 14-line poem, often about love

3. Poetry often pays a lot of attention to the sounds of words. Rhymes at the ends of lines are usually easy to spot, but picking out sounds that go together within a line can be more difficult. Read the following line aloud and listen to the sounds:

   If the p<u>i</u>nes and the l<u>i</u>mes wr<u>i</u>te l<u>i</u>nes that rh<u>y</u>me

   The vowels that sound alike are underlined. This is called assonance. Write out the following lines, say them aloud, then underline the similar vowel sounds.

   if the hickory's trick is the limerick
   if the ash can bash out a sonnet
   if the elm excels at villanelles
   if the yew does a cool haiku

4. This is a shape poem. Think of five other shapes that might make good frames for a poem. Suggest a subject for each shape.

5. Write your own shape poem. If you are stuck for how to start, the word 'if' may help.

Check your learning

Check that you understand the words you have been learning: limerick, shape poem, sonnet, haiku, free verse, metaphor, simile, pun, assonance. Make a note of any you need help with.
Look at each other's shape poems. Talk about how you think the shape and the words work together. What could be improved?

Learning extra

Look back at 'Little Acorns' to see how many rhyming words you can find. List them, splitting them into words that rhyme completely and words that nearly rhyme.

Facing the truth – with Haikus

Malorie Blackman

Your learning

In this poem, Malorie Blackman writes about a classroom disagreement. Here you will study and comment on how the poet creates a sense of the situation through the two main characters in the poem.

EXPLANATIONS

haiku a three-line poem, originally from Japan. The first and third lines have five syllables each, the second line has seven

Facing the truth – with Haikus

Mr Mackie said,
'Today you lucky people,
We're doing haikus!'

'What's one of them, sir?'
5 'Poems to stir the senses,
Plus, they're very short.

A mere three lines long
Just seventeen syllables
Simple, pimple – right?

10 Three lines made up of
Words which are five syllables
Then seven, then five.'

'Haikus,' Alex groaned.
'What a waste of time and space.'
15 I didn't think so.

'Japanese poems.
Haikus ...' sighed Mr Mackie.
'A pure, paced rhythm.'

'But sir,' said Alex,
20 'Haikus mean lots of counting.
That's not fair! That's maths!'

'Haikus are art, child,
Full of heart, soul and passion
So let your mind soar.'

25 'To where? And what for?'
'To the stars and beyond, child.'
'And when I land, sir?'

Mr Mackie frowned,
Scratched his head and frowned some more.
30 'You'll have memories.'

'Big deal!' Alex scoffed.
And that was the end of that.
Haikus bit the dust.

35 *Haiku for Davey:*
We should've been friends
But the bad thing that happened
To you changed my life.

1. Narrative poetry tells a story. In this poem, we are introduced to Mr Mackie and Alex. What is your initial impression of the relationship between them?

2. What do you discover about Mr Mackie in this poem? Look first at the opinions below.
   - He's got a sense of humour.
   - He enjoys rhyme.
   - He wants the work to sound easy.
   - He gives up rather quickly.
   - He likes imagination.
   - He uses alliteration.
   - He's a dreamer.

   Find evidence for five of these and set it out like the table below. The first one is done for you.

Opinion	Evidence
He's got a sense of humour	The way he calls the students 'you lucky people' suggests he is being light-hearted. He knows it's a lesson, not a special treat

3. Write two short statements about Alex and find evidence to support them.

4. Each stanza in the poem is a haiku. Why do you think the poet chose to write the poem this way?

5. The last stanza is a bit of a mystery and has its own subtitle. What explanations can you think of for its being there? Consider:
   - who Davey might be
   - what might have happened
   - how this could link up with Mr Mackie's lesson.

6. What have you discovered about the characters in this poem? Write two paragraphs about what it would be like to be in this English class. Provide evidence for the points you are making.

Check your learning

In pairs, listen to what your partner has written about the characters in the poem. Talk about where you agree and whether your evidence is similar or different. Choose the point in each other's work that is best supported by evidence.

Learning extra

Try writing a haiku about people or things. Here's one about a radio:

It can speak to you
And be music in your ears
But you can't talk back!

Linking the *Playing with words* poems

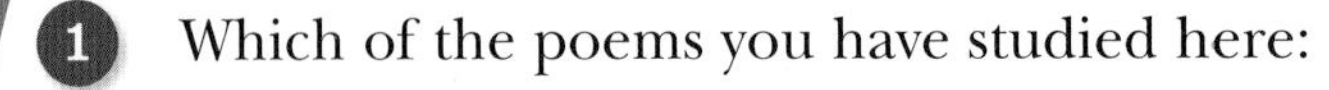

Your learning

The poems in this section are about experimenting with words and poetic forms. Here, you will experiment with words yourself and find out about rhythm.

1 Which of the poems you have studied here:

a is a shape poem
b uses the haiku form
c includes many of the words used to describe poems
d deals with the oddities of the English language
e has a conversation in it
f uses rhyme?

2 When two or more closely connected words start with the same sound, it is called alliteration. Here's an example from 'Why English is so Hard':

But the plural of house is houses, not hice.

a Write out one example of alliteration from each of the three poems, with the alliteration marked as it is in the example above.
b What is the effect of the alliteration in each poem?

information

Syllable
a single beat or sound in a word: e.g. 'hit' has one syllable and 'hitting' has two.

3 In this section you have seen how words work together through rhyme, shape, syllable pattern and the repetition of sounds. Rhythm is another way in which words can be linked. Rhythm is the pattern of stresses in language; it is mainly used in poetry and song, and is most easily understood by looking at examples. Look at these two lines:

The play is there upon the page:
It's not alive until on stage.

The pattern is for every second syllable to be stressed. It is what some people call a 'de-dum, de-dum' rhythm, but its formal name is iambic metre.

Copy and complete these two iambic lines using the spare words beside them.

The stage is where...	can	sing	words	the
For any...	listening		who	are

4 When you stress the first syllable, you get a rhythm that is called dactylic, for example:

Shambles, mumbles, fickle, sniggle,
Bluster, fluster, gaggle, giggle.

Create two more dactylic lines using some of the words below. Watch out – not all of them will work!

gutter	batter
waffle	piffle
booting	shooting
alive	about
sparkle	silly
chilli	trickle
tickle	trifle
stifle	trick
speak	natter
table	top

5 Now write your own poem, using language in one or more of the ways you have studied here. You have looked at:

- rhythm
- rhyme
- alliteration
- assonance
- shape poetry
- haiku
- characters in conversation.

Step one

Choose a subject or idea that is connected with words and the way we use them. Here are some examples:

- phrases that parents use
- the language that teachers use to settle a class down
- words on favourite subjects – e.g. football, fashion, film, fishing
- words that sound good together
- words to help you cope with loneliness
- things you say to cheer up your friends.

Step two

Decide on the form you are going to use. You will need to decide whether to write in stanzas or not. Try to use some of the things listed in question 5 above. Here are three examples:

Fashion victim
bits of glitter, sticks together
wears too little in all weather

Lesson Haiku
settle down now please
I will not ask you again
It's my last warning

L8
'What time do you call this?'
I look down at my feet.
'My watch isn't working.'
'You've said that before.'
She stares straight at me.
'I think it's the battery.'

Step three

Write the first draft of your poem.

Check your learning

Read your poem to a partner. Have they used any of the kinds of writing you have studied in this section?
What part of your writing are you most pleased with?
Work with your partner to improve any parts you are not happy with.

Learning extra

Write another piece that focuses on the words of a subject that interests you, such as music, pets, sport, hobbies. You can use one of the poetry forms you have studied here, or choose another form that suits what you want to say.

It's not unusual for one poet to imitate the style of another; you may have done this yourself when writing a poem.
Here, you will examine an entertaining example of this.

Jabberwocky

Lewis Carroll

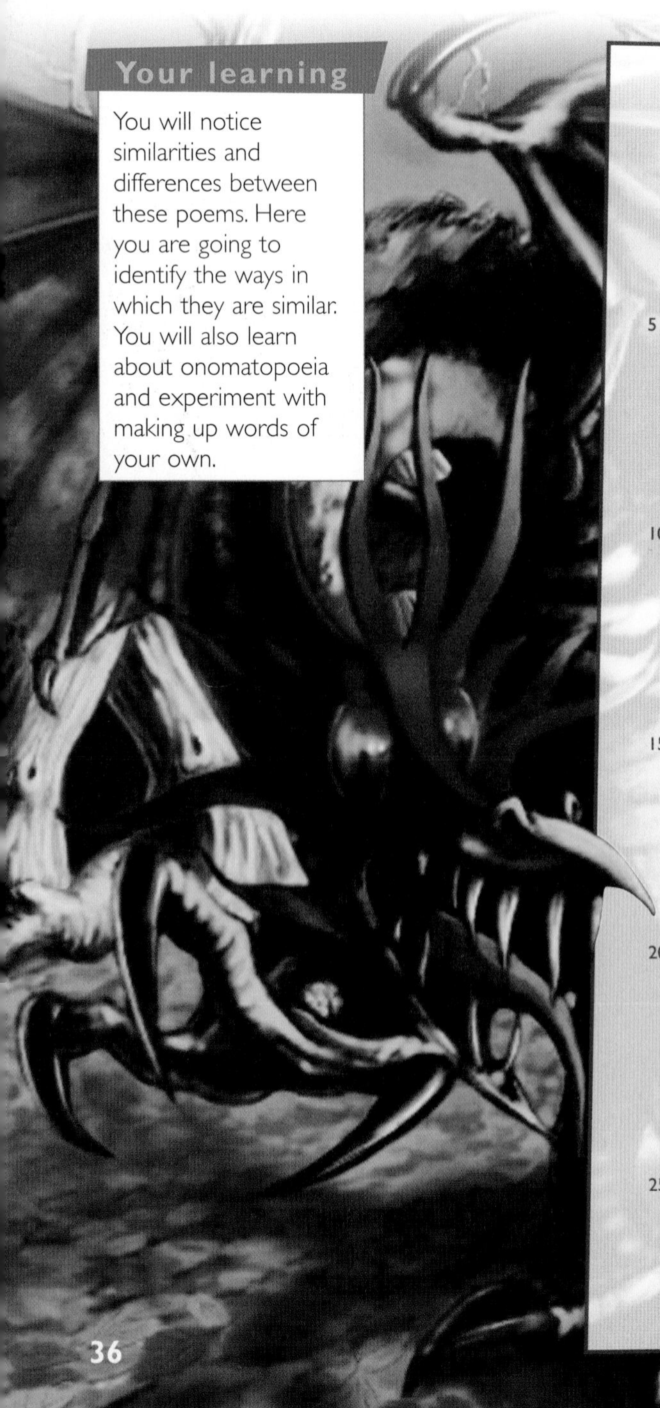

Your learning

You will notice similarities and differences between these poems. Here you are going to identify the ways in which they are similar. You will also learn about onomatopoeia and experiment with making up words of your own.

Jabberwocky

'Twas brillig, and the slithy toves
Did gyre and gimble in the wabe;
All mimsy were the borogroves
And the mome raths outgrabe.

5 'Beware the Jabberwock, my son!
The jaws that bite, the claws that catch!
Beware the Jubjub bird, and shun
The frumious Bandersnatch!'

He took his vorpal sword in hand:
10 Long time the manxome foe he sought –
So rested he by the Tumtum tree,
And stood awhile in thought.

And as in uffish thought he stood,
The Jabberwock, with eyes of flame,
15 Came whiffling through the tulgey wood,
And burbled as it came!

One, two! One, two! And through and through
The vorpal blade went snicker-snack!
He left it dead, and with its head
20 He went galumphing back.

'And hast thou slain the Jabberwock?
Come to my arms, my beamish boy!
O frabjous day! Callooh! Callay!'
He chortled in his joy.

25 'Twas brillig, and the slithy toves
Did gyre and gimble in the wabe;
All mimsy were the borogroves,
And the mome raths outgrabe.

Jabbermockery

TREVOR MILLUM

Jabbermockery

Twas Thursday and the bottom set
Did gyre and gimble in the gym.
All mimsy was Miss Borogrove
And the Head of Maths was grim.

5 *Beware the Mathematix, my friend!*
His sums that snarl, his coordinates that catch!
Beware the Deputy-Bird, and shun
The evil Earring-Snatch!

She took her ballpoint pen in hand:
10 Longtime the problem's end she sought –
So rested she by the lavatory
And sat a while in thought.

And as in toughish thought she sat,
The Mathematix with eyes of flame
15 Came calculating through the cloakroom doors
And subtracted as he came!

She thought real fast as he went past;
The well-placed soap went slickersmack!
She left him stunned and with the sums
20 She went galumphing back.

And hast thou got the answers, Jackie?
Come to our desk, beamed idle boys,
Oh, frabjous day! Quelle heure! Calais!
They chortled in their joy.

25 Twas Thursday and the bottom set
Did gyre and gimble in the gym.
All mimsy was Miss Borogrove
And the Head of Maths was grim.

1. In 'Jabberwocky' the poet uses made-up words to create an imaginary world, but it is still possible to make sense of the poem. Think about:
   - what the words suggest to you
   - how the words are used in the sentence.

   Rewrite the first stanza, replacing the made-up words with actual words that you think would make sense. Compare your version with a partner's and talk about why you chose the words you did. There are no right or wrong answers.

2. **a** In pairs, read the rest of the poem and decide what each stanza means. You will need to look at individual lines.

   b Write your own dictionary definitions for the words below. The first one has been done for you. Remember, there is no right or wrong answer.

   frumious: *adjective*, frightening, horribly scary
   Bandersnatch:
   vorpal:
   manxome:
   whiffling:
   tulgey:
   frabjous:

3. 'Jabbermockery' is a comic imitation, or parody, of Lewis Carroll's famous poem. It is set in a real rather than an imaginary world.

   a What is the setting for 'Jabbermockery'? How do you know this?

   b Make a table like the one below to show the ways 'Jabbermockery' imitates 'Jabberwocky'.

Jabberwocky	*Jabbermockery*
the slithy toves	the bottom set
the borogroves	Miss Borogrove
mome raths	Head of Maths
Jabberwock	...

   c With a partner, talk about how your reading of 'Jabbermockery' was affected by your reading of 'Jabberwocky'. For example, you might say: 'Now I understand why the poem rhymes the way it does.' To get you started, you might want to talk about:
   - humour
   - the characters.

4 Sometimes made-up words become real words. You can find *galumph* in the dictionary, defined as follows:

> **galumph** (*say* gal-umf) verb to prance or leap triumphantly.
> (from GAL(lop) + (tri)UMPH, coined by Lewis Carroll in 1871)

New words are added to the dictionary all the time, for example 'humungous', which means 'extremely large'. How do you think this word was created?

a Now have a go at inventing words of your own. You could join existing words or create entirely new ones.

b In pairs or small groups, look at your made-up words and choose the best ones.

5 **a** Sometimes writers use letters to reproduce sounds exactly, for example *aaaaaarrgh!, hoorah!, shhh…, ow!, ouch!* Where does Lewis Carroll do this in 'Jabberwocky'?

b At other times writers may use words, real or made-up, to suggest the sound of the noise or action being described. This is called onomatopoeia. Say the word *gal-umph-ing*. Does it suggest a quiet or loud noise, a heavy or soft movement? Which part of the movement is the heaviest – the start, the middle or the end?

c Find the following onomatopoeic words in 'Jabberwocky' and 'Jabbermockery':

burbled **snicker-snack** **slickersmack** **chortled**

How well do you think they suggest the noise or action they describe?

d Make a list of other onomatopoeic words that you know. Here are two to start you off: **hiss** **slither**

Check your learning

Now that you've read about the Jabberwock and the Mathematix, it's your turn.

a Draw a strange-looking creature in the centre of a blank piece of paper – just a quick sketch, don't spend too long on it.

b Invent a name for your creature.

c Make up words that could be used to describe:

- its appearance
- the things it does
- the way it moves
- the noises it makes.

d Write your made-up words around your creature.

e Now work in a group. Show your creature to the others and read out your words exactly as you want them to be said.

f As a group, decide which words are the most interesting.

g Using what you have learnt from your discussion, add to your words for your own creature.

Learning extra

Write a poem or the opening paragraph of a story about your imaginary creature. Use as many made-up words as you can, so that your readers have to use their imagination.

Benjamin Zephaniah was born in Birmingham and now lives in East London. A lot of his writing is influenced by the music and poetry of Jamaica. In this section, you will get a sense of how he can write both passionately and personally. You'll be looking at three very different poems by him, discovering how they contrast with each other and have similarities.

Wot a pair

BENJAMIN ZEPHANIAH

Your learning

Many people find it hard to know what to say about humorous poetry, apart from whether it made them laugh or not. Here you will explore a range of techniques used by the poet to make the poem humorous.

Wot a pair

I waz walking down Wyefront street
When me trousers ran away,
I waz feeling incomplete
But still me trousers would not stay
5 When I found where they had gone
De pair addressed me rather blunt,
And they told me they were sick of being put on
Back to front.

I told dem I would treat dem good
10 And wear dem back to back,
I promised dem protection
From a friend who is a mac,
Me trousers did not believe a single word I had to say,
And me underpants were laughing
15 When me trousers ran away.

1. What sort of picture does this poem create in your mind?

2. The most important thing about humorous poems in general is that they are fun. List three details that show that this is a humorous poem rather than a serious one.

   Explain how one of the examples you have chosen adds to the humour.

   You could begin:

   'Wyefront Street' adds to the humour because...

3. Surprise is also an important part of humour. Choose one surprising event or action from the poem. Say why you weren't expecting it and why it adds to the humour.

4. The poet's use of personification also adds to the humour in this poem. The personification is the pair of trousers that speaks and acts like a human being.

   a Describe the way the trousers treat the narrator and how the narrator reacts.

   b How would you sum up the relationship between the trousers and the narrator?

information

Personification

This is when something that is not human is given human characteristics, e.g. the moon looked down and smiled to see their laughter.

5. Write two paragraphs about the poem. You could start the first one with the words:
   'What is unusual about this Benjamin Zephaniah poem...'

   You could start the second paragraph with:
   'The poem is humorous because...'

   You could write about:

   - the unexpected things that happen in the poem
   - the effect of the talking trousers
   - your favourite parts of the poem.

Check your learning

- Read the paragraphs you wrote for question 5 to a partner.
- Choose one good point from your partner's paragraphs. Explain to your partner why you like it.
- Discuss what kind of person you think this poem might appeal to.

Learning extra

Write your own humorous poem in which something (a wallet, trainers, a bag, a teeth brace, a football, socks, a toothbrush, a hat) complains about the way you've been treating it.

According to my mood

BENJAMIN ZEPHANIAH

Your learning

Poets often enjoy using language in imaginative or unusual ways as they break with conventions. Here you will look at how Benjamin Zephaniah uses language, then comment on what he is doing and how successful he is.

According to my mood

I have poetic licence, i wriTe thE way i waNt.
i drop my full stops where i like…
MY CAPITAL LeteRs go where i liKE,
i order from MY PeN, i verse the way i like
5 (i do my spelling write)
According to My MOod.
i HAve Poetic licence,
i put commers where i like,,((0).
(((my brackets are write((
10 I REPEAT WHen i likE.
i can't go rong.
i look and i.c.
It's rite.
il REPEAT WHen i likE. i have
15 poetic licence!
don't question me????

1. Read the poem aloud in several ways. You could try:
   - aggressively
   - politely
   - with a smile in your voice.

   Which seems best suited to the poem? Why?

2. Choose three things about this poem that are unusual or unexpected. Discuss why they are unusual or unexpected. What is their effect on the reader?

3. Understanding the poet's attitude can help you understand the poem as a whole. Find evidence or quotations from this poem to support each of the statements in the table below. Copy and complete the table, then decide what you think is the most likely attitude of the poet in this poem.

Attitude	Evidence
he doesn't care	
he's having fun	
he's playing with language	
he's challenging people to think about language	
he's raising questions	

4. Poetry is not the only form of writing that uses language creatively. Text messages and e-mails often break writing conventions. With a partner, list examples of text messages and e-mails that include unusual uses of:
   - shortened words or contractions, for example *tmb*, *2nite*, *gr8*
   - capital letters
   - punctuation.

5. Sometimes people are not happy about unusual or creative spelling and punctuation. Discuss and make notes with a partner on how you would answer someone who says Benjamin Zephaniah's poem is no good because it's full of 'mistakes'. You can use the work you have done in the previous questions to help you. You could also think about:
   - different ways language is used, for example, in texting and e-mails
   - different attitudes that people have to how language is used
   - whether poetry is different from other forms of writing.

Check your learning

- List the three most important things that you think someone needs to understand in order to appreciate this poem.
- Compare your answer with a partner's.

Learning extra

Try writing about having a licence for food just as Benjamin Zephaniah does for language. Write about eating what you like, when you like, where you like and how you like. Be different and be eyecatching.

Important notice

BENJAMIN ZEPHANIAH

Your learning

Poets sometimes have viewpoints to get across. Here you will look at how Benjamin Zephaniah communicates his viewpoint and the effect it has on the reader.

Important notice

Careful what you do
careful what you say,
don't bow down to them
and never go astray,
careful what you eat (5)
watch where you put your feet,
for in this dirty scene
a man must try live clean.

Corruption walks with smiling faces
when they're out their hiding places. (10)

Silence glows and makes no sound
some will try to keep you down.

So walk with a watchful eye
for man don't fear to die,
stand with an upright stance (15)
don't fear them and their sentence.

Careful what you do
careful what you say,
don't think of great profit
take what's yours and go your way, (20)
look forward and behind
for in dark place you find,
the ones who cut you off
will do so and then laugh,
seek and you will find (25)
don't let them blow your mind,
try to do your best
don't welcome unwanted guest.

Corruption walks with smiling faces
when they're out their hiding places. (30)

Silence glows and makes no sound
some will try to keep you down.

EXPLANATIONS

corruption dishonesty or loss of innocence

1 Imperatives tell people what to do. They are commands, warnings, requests or advice, e.g. *Sit down.* *Be careful.* *Don't be cruel.*

Imperatives are a direct way of communicating with someone.

a Write down the first imperative in this poem.
Does this sound more like a request or a warning to you?

b How many imperatives can you find altogether in this poem?

c What do you think is the effect of there being so many?

2 Repetition is often used in writing or speaking, in order to emphasise the point being made. It draws attention to the words and increases the sense of their importance. It also makes the reader more likely to think carefully about their meaning.

Several lines are repeated in this poem. Copy and complete the table below, to help your understanding of why the poet has included repeated lines.

Lines repeated	Effect of repetition

3 Often the title of the poem is the key to understanding what the poem is about. To help your understanding of what 'Important notice' is about:

- divide into small groups or pairs and choose an eight-line section of the poem
- discuss and make notes on all of the important notice points in your section
- as a class, pool together all your findings.

4 Write two or three short paragraphs about what Benjamin Zephaniah is saying in this poem and how he communicates that effectively. You could:

- sum up in a sentence or two what the poem is saying
- write about the effect of using imperatives and repetitions
- write about how the way the poem is written relates to what the poet is trying to say.

Check your learning

- In pairs, tell each other what imperatives are and give two examples each.
- Explain to each other how imperatives and repetitions help this poem to come alive.
- Explain to each other how the imperatives and repetition relate to what the poem is about.

Learning extra

Write ten points of advice to help parents cope with teenagers. Put your points in your own speaking voice as Benjamin Zephaniah does. You could start: *Don't say things if you don't mean them. It makes teenagers…*

Linking the Benjamin Zephaniah poems

Your learning

Here you will be looking again at the three Benjamin Zephaniah poems on pages 40–44. You will compare the poems, coming to a judgement about what qualities they have and what is distinctive about this poet.

1 Benjamin Zephaniah is an out-of-the-ordinary poet. To help your understanding of what makes his poems distinctive, choose four words from the list below for each of the three poems.

firm	funny	furious	statement
warning	story	experiment	fantasy
advice	playing	joking	teaching

2 What links the three poems? Copy the diagram below and write in the statements that you think link the poems together. Six choices are given below the diagram, but feel free to add suggestions of your own.

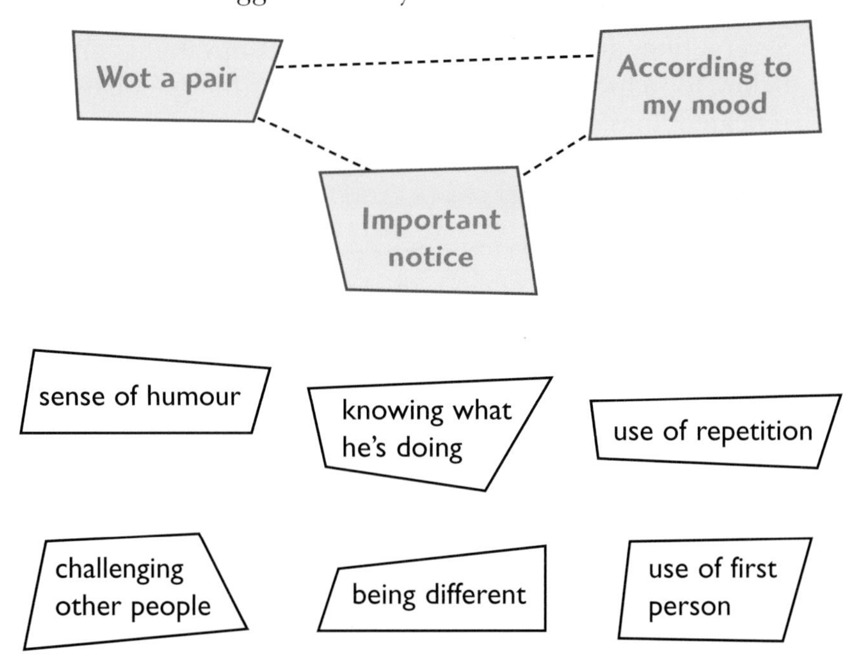

3 In groups or as a class, copy the table below. List the effective points about each poem; say why you think they are good and give reasons.

Wot a pair	It exaggerates the scene like cartoons do.
According to my mood	
Important notice	

4 What clues do you think the poems give about the man who wrote them? Write three sentences about Benjamin Zephaniah as you imagine him. For everything you say, find something in a poem that supports your idea. Refer to the poem using short quotations where possible, e.g.

I think Benjamin Zephaniah is aware that his job is being a poet. That's why he starts 'According to my mood' by saying 'I have poetic licence'.

Share what you have written with a partner. Talk about the similarities and differences in your views.

5 Write a short introduction to Benjamin Zephaniah's poetry for a group of 11–12-year-old pupils who are about to read these three poems. Use the ideas and evidence you have collected through the previous four questions. Aim to write three paragraphs. You could include comments on:

- the variety to be found in his poems
- his sense of humour
- his strongly-held views.

Check your learning

- Read your introductions to Benjamin Zephaniah to each other.
- Write down one point about the poet that you gained from listening to each other.
- What have you learnt about how the way the poet writes relates to what he wants to write about?
- How has this section helped you get a clearer picture of these poems and the man who wrote them?

Learning extra

What would you want to ask Benjamin Zephaniah if you met him? Look back over the three poems and come up with 10–15 questions you could ask him in an interview. Use general questions in the first part and specific ones about the poems you have read in the second part.

'Poetry is language at its most rich. Poetry can surprise and astonish ... When you read poetry you realise that there are many multiple meanings in a single short poem. Poetry provokes discussion and argument. Poetry inhabits ideas better than any other form. Poetry stands the test of time.'
Jackie Kay, Poetryclass, *TES*

English Cousin comes to Scotland

JACKIE KAY

Your learning

In this poem Jackie Kay writes in the first person, as though she were telling the reader a personal story. Here you will investigate how she uses non-standard English to help create a sense of speaking directly to the reader.

English Cousin comes to Scotland

See when my English cousin comes,
it's so embarrassing so it is, so it is.
I have to explain everything
I mean Every Thing, so I do, so I do.
5 I told her, 'know what happened to me?
I got skelped, because I screamed when a skelf
went into my pinky finger: OUCH, loud.
And ma ma dropped her best bit of china.
It wis sore, so it wis, so it wis.
10 I was scunnert being skelped
when I wis already sore.
So I ran and ran, holding
my pinky, through the park,
over the burn, up the hill.
15 I was knackered and I fell
into the mud and went home
mocket and got skelped again.
So I locked myself in the cludgie
and cried, so I did, so I did,
20 pulling the long roll of paper
onto the floor. Like that dug Andrex.'
Whilst I'm saying this, my English cousin
has her mouth open. Glaikit.
Stupit. So she is, so she is.
25 I says, 'I'm going to have to learn you
what's what.' And at that the wee git
cheers up; the wee toffee nose says,
'not learn you, teach you,' like she's scored.

EXPLANATIONS

burn a small stream

1. In this poem Jackie Kay writes in Scottish dialect. Dialect is the type of regional English spoken in a particular area. Make a list of any words you do not recognise in the poem. With a partner, try to work out what the words mean, using the parts you do understand to help you.

2. Here are some of the dialect words used in the poem. Check your understanding of these words by matching them to their correct meaning:

cludgie	splinter
glaikit	small
mocket	smacked
skelf	annoyed
skelped	toilet
scunnert	dirty
wee	looking confused

3. Write down three reasons why the poet might have chosen to write in dialect. Think about:
   - how it helps to recreate speech
   - the pictures dialect creates in the mind of the reader
   - what the use of dialect tells you about the poet.

4. As well as using dialect words to create a sense of speaking directly to the reader, the poet uses slang: non-standard words in common use. Examples of these in the poem are *git,* meaning fool or unpleasant person and *toffee nose,* meaning snob. Think about the way you speak with friends. List and explain the slang words you use most often.

5. The poet uses repetition, for example: *it's so embarrassing so it is, so it is.*

   a Write down as many other examples of repetition as you can find in this poem.

   b One reason why the poet uses repetition is because she wants to create the rhythms of real speech.
   Think of two more reasons and write them down.

Check your learning

List the different methods Jackie Kay uses to create a sense of speaking directly to the reader. For each one, explain its effect on you as a reader. Compare your answers with a partner's.

Learning extra

Write 5–10 lines of a typical conversation you might have with a friend. Highlight and annotate any use of the first person, dialect, slang and repetition.

Tomorrow they'll be coming to get me

JACKIE KAY

Your learning

Poets don't always speak directly to the reader. Sometimes they adopt a different *voice* or *persona*. Here, you will explore how the poet adopts an unusual *voice* to give more force to her ideas.

Tomorrow they'll be coming to get me

This isn't paranoia. This is experience.
I've just watched my pals go one by one.
We used to dance all together
with our friends that have been moved
5 out of their homes. Now new ones have come
with their long faces. White faces.
We are getting done in for a pound of beef
a wardrobe, a letter, a roll of toilet paper.
We did mount protests. Sit-in-the-forest-
10 don't-budge kind of thing. But we're no match
for those big machetes. They don't care.
Basically. We're not Burnham Woods either.
We can't just up and off to a nicer spot.
Then again, we've been here hundreds of years.
15 Tomorrow it is another story. Chop. Tomorrow
after that, chop chop, and so it will go on
until we are all done. But then.
There will be floods like Noah never imagined.
Bright blinding lights. The earth's skin
20 burnt to tatters. Mark my words.
This is a dangerous game they're playing.

EXPLANATIONS

a pound of beef trees are sometimes cut down to make way for cattle which are more profitable

paranoia a fear of something when there is no need to be afraid

Burnham Woods in Shakespeare's play *Macbeth* soldiers cut branches off the trees in Burnham Wood to disguise their advance on Macbeth's castle. It looked as though the forest was moving

1 With a partner, talk about who, or what, you think the *voice* in this poem belongs to.

a If you agree, list at least three reasons why you think this. If you do not agree, list your reasons separately and then decide whose are the more convincing.

b Identify the point in the poem when you were certain you knew what or who the voice belonged to. What made you certain?

2 What does the voice tell you about:

- the things that are happening to its home
- the reasons why the trees are being destroyed
- the people who are cutting down the trees
- the things that will happen when all the trees have been destroyed?

3 The poet wrote her poem using the voice of a tree in the forest. Here are some reasons which may explain why she did this. Place them in order, putting the most important one first. If you think of any others, add them to the list.

a It presents a puzzle for the reader to work out.

b It lets the reader see things from the point of view of a tree.

c It makes what is happening seem more real.

d It lets the poet write about things she couldn't say directly to the reader.

e It makes the reader think more carefully about what is going on.

Explain the reasons for your order to a partner.

4 Write between three and five sentences explaining what you think about the destruction of the rainforests, basing your ideas on what you have read in the poem.

Check your learning

- Using what you have learnt about the use of a voice in a poem, copy and complete these sentences:

  A poet might use a different voice in a poem to…

  The use of a different voice can help the reader to … and …
- Compare your completed sentences with a partner's.

Learning extra

Write a poem using the voice of one of the following:

- **a house** that is being destroyed to make way for a new road
- **an elephant** that is being hunted for its ivory tusks
- **a toy** that is being thrown out because a child has got too old for it.

Pollution

JACKIE KAY

Your learning

In this poem Jackie Kay writes in the third person. Here you will examine how she uses *personification* and *structure* to present her ideas on pollution.

Pollution

Only when everyone in West Green Road
has gone to sleep: when every Doberman
has stopped barking, every ghetto blaster
stopped blasting and all the tom cats
5 have stopped fighting, does she walk the street
under the yellow light of the streetlamps.

She wears a silver sweatshirt and a brand new
pair of trainers; the huge tongue licks her toes.
With her busy brush and her dustpan dan she goes
10 through mounds of wrappers and applecores,
cans and empty cartons of milk, banana skins
and bottle tops. Munch into the big mouth.

She is fast and furious and very fit.
The anger in her eyes is a brilliant torch.
15 Passing each shop she tries to make up
a rap, but the drains and sewers, Drip drip,
make her feel she's a born loser, Rat tat.
Tomorrow they'll still be drinking dirty water.

EXPLANATIONS

West Green Road a main road in north London, but typical of many main roads

ghetto blaster a portable stereo system taking its name from poor inner-city neighbourhoods known as ghettos

1 *Personification* is when an animal or object is described as if it were human. Jackie Kay personifies a mechanical roadsweeper.

a In which line is the roadsweeper first mentioned? What word does the poet use to refer to it?

b List all the things you are told about the roadsweeper.

> she walks the streets
> she wears a silver sweatshirt

c Share your list with a partner. Add any details you have missed. Sort your final list into three groups: how the roadsweeper looks; what it does; how it feels.

d Suggest three reasons why the poet made a roadsweeping machine the central character in a poem about pollution.

2 The word *structure* refers to the ways a poem is organised. With a partner, decide whether the following statements are true or false:

a 'Pollution' is organised in three stanzas.

b The first stanza sets the scene.

c The first and the last lines of the poem are about people.

d The first and the last lines of the poem are about rats.

e The second stanza is about the people who live in this place.

f The second stanza is about the appearance and actions of the machine.

g The third stanza is about the feelings of the roadsweeping machine.

h Every stanza is about pollution.

Check your answers with another pair. Talk about any differences you have and make changes if needed.

3 Re-read the poem. With a partner, discuss and make notes on the things this poem tells you about pollution. Talk about:

- what you learn about the place
- the machine's actions and feelings
- the last line of the poem.

Check your learning

List three things you have learnt about each of the following:

- the use of personification in this poem
- the ways the ideas are structured.

Compare your answers with a partner's.

Learning extra

Use your notes from question 3 to help you write an answer to the question: What do you think the poet thinks and feels about pollution?

For each point you make, explain why you think it and refer to the poem.

Linking the Jackie Kay poems

Your learning

Here you will be looking again at the three Jackie Kay poems on pages 48–52. You will explore the links between the titles and the poems, the ideas that underpin the poems and the different ways the poet structures her ideas. You will be thinking, talking and writing about two or three poems together.

1. Think about the titles of the three poems: 'English Cousin comes to Scotland', 'Tomorrow they'll be coming to get me' and 'Pollution'. Talk with a partner about:
   - what each title suggests to you
   - how each title links with its poem
   - which title you think is best and why.

2. Choose the poem that you think has the best title. Using your discussion from question 1 to help you, write two or three sentences to follow on from each of these starters:

   The title ... makes me think about...

   The title links with the poem in a number of ways...

   I think this is the best title because...

3. The word *structure* refers to the way a poem is organised. Remind yourself of the work you did on the structure of 'Pollution' on page 52. Now look at 'English Cousin comes to Scotland' and 'Tomorrow they'll be coming to get me'. Match each of the following statements to the correct poem or poems.

   a This poem has no stanzas.
   b This poem starts and ends in a similar way.
   c This poem records a past conversation.
   d This poem uses repetition to link ideas and imitate speech.
   e This poem starts in the present, moves to the past, then to the present, then to the future and ends in the present.
   f This poem tells a story about something that has happened.
   g This poem reflects on something that is happening.

4. 'Pollution' and 'Tomorrow they'll be coming to get me' are both about the environment. Copy and complete the tables below by matching the quotations on the following page with the appropriate comment. This will help you identify what Jackie Kay is saying about the environment.

Quotation	Comment
when every Doberman has stopped barking, every ghetto blaster stopped blasting and all the tom cats have stopped fighting	The poet draws our attention to the noise pollution that is all around us.

	Quotations
A	*We are getting done in for a pound of beef a wardrobe, a letter, a roll of toilet paper*
B	*But we're no match for those big machetes. They don't care.*
C	*Tomorrow after that, chop chop, and so it will go on until we are all done.*
D	*There will be floods like Noah never imagined.*
E	*This is a dangerous game they're playing.*
F	*she goes through mounds of wrappers and applecores, cans and empty cartons of milk, banana skins and bottle tops.*
G	*But the drains and sewers, Drip drip, make her feel she's a born loser.*
H	*Tomorrow they'll still be drinking dirty water.*

	Comments
1	The destruction of the rainforests will have serious consequences.
2	Humans have got to take the environment seriously.
3	No matter how much litter you clear, there will be more the next day.
4	Trees are being destroyed for worthless things.
5	Trying to fight the litter problem is a depressing task.
6	Trees are not able to defend themselves against humans.
7	Humans won't stop until they have destroyed all the trees.
8	There is all kinds of litter on our streets.

5 Poetry can make us think about things we haven't thought about before, or can develop our thinking further. Talk with a partner, or in a small group, about the problems of pollution and the destruction of the rainforests. Make a list of five things you think people could do to help solve these problems. Use what you have learnt from the poems and your own ideas.

Check your learning

What have you learnt about the following from studying these poems:

- the links between a poem's title and the poem itself
- the different ways Jackie Kay structures her ideas
- the types of things Jackie Kay chooses to write about?

Write your answers and compare them with a partner's. Talk about any differences you have. Add to your answers after your discussion.

Learning extra

Choose a subject you feel strongly about, and list at least three points you would want to make about it in a poem. Think about:

- what technique(s) would be best to get your points across to the reader: personification/adopting a different voice/using dialect
- how you could structure your poem: stanzas/free verse/chronologically
- the title you would choose.

Write your poem. Decide whether to keep or change your chosen title.

William Blake was born in 1757, the third son of a London sock maker. His poems often challenged the thinking and behaviour of rich people and the church of his day. In this section, you will study three poems that give you a sense of how Blake looked at the world.

The Tyger

William Blake

Your learning

Poets use a variety of techniques to bring their subjects alive for the reader. Here you will explore how Blake brings the tiger to life and what impression that gives you of what the poet was thinking.

The Tyger

Tyger, Tyger, burning bright,
In the forests of the night;
What immortal hand or eye,
Could frame thy fearful symmetry?

5 In what distant deeps or skies,
Burnt the fire of thine eyes?
On what wings dare he aspire?
What the hand dare seize the fire?

And what shoulder, and what art,
10 Could twist the sinews of thy heart?
And when thy heart began to beat,
What dread hand? and what dread feet?

What the hammer? what the chain?
In what furnace was thy brain?
15 What the anvil? what dread grasp,
Dare its deadly terrors clasp?
When the stars threw down their spears
And watered heaven with their tears:
Did he smile his work to see?
20 Did he who made the Lamb make thee?

Tyger Tyger, burning bright,
In the forests of the night:
What immortal hand or eye,
Dare frame thy fearful symmetry?

EXPLANATIONS

immortal living forever
aspire climb higher
sinews muscles or power
thy/thine your
furnace a very hot place, usually for melting metals
anvil a block for hammering metal objects into shape
thee you

1 **a** What initial impression do you get of the tiger in this poem?

b Choose five words from the list below that you feel best convey your impression, and rank them in order with the best first.

spooky	*strong*	*powerful*	*menacing*
different	*strange*	*mythical*	*fantastic*
sinister	*magical*	*wonderful*	*scary*
mysterious	*great*	*terrifying*	*dangerous*

c Explain why each of your five words is best for describing the tiger.

2 Blake uses a number of sound patterns in this poem, including alliteration, repetition and rhyme.

a With a partner, find and list:

- two examples of alliteration
- three examples of repetition
- four examples of internal rhyme.

b Discuss what you feel is the overall effect of including all these sound features in this poem.

3 The poet is not just describing a tiger – he is writing about the making of the tiger. Find evidence in the poem to prove this. For example, look at lines 13–15.

4 None of the questions in the poem is about the tiger; they are all about the creator of the tiger. Re-read the poem, then:

a List all the questions in the poem.

b For each question, explain what you think the poet is asking.

c Overall, what do you think the poet is worried about?

5 What have you learnt about the making of the tiger and what William Blake is writing about in this poem? Write two paragraphs and try to include quotations to prove the points you are making.

information

Alliteration

This is the repetition of the same sound at the beginning of two or more words, e.g. the frightened fox. *The words may be next to or very near each other.*

information

Internal rhyme

This is the repetition of a sound within a line or between lines.

Check your learning

- In pairs, tell each other what you understand about this poem and what pictures it brings to mind.
- Talk about what the sound patterns add to the poem.
- Talk about what you have understood best about this poem.

Learning extra

Write about the creation of a frightening creature. It can be real (e.g. shark, lion, hawk) or imaginary (e.g. gryphon, orc). Try to get the sense of someone creating this creature.

Holy Thursday

WILLIAM BLAKE

Your learning

This poem is about the procession of poor children to an annual church service for Charity schools. Many people praised the schools but they were often brutal places. Here you will identify how Blake saw this aspect of his society and explore the way in which he communicates this.

Holy Thursday

Is this a holy thing to see,
In a rich and fruitful land,
Babes reduced to misery,
Fed with cold and usurous hand?

5 Is that trembling cry a song?
Can it be a song of joy?
And so many children poor?
It is a land of poverty!

And their sun does never shine,
10 And their fields are bleak and bare.
And their ways are fill'd with thorns
It is eternal winter there.

For where-e'er the sun does shine,
And where-e'er the rain does fall:
15 Babe can never hunger there,
Nor poverty the mind appall.

EXPLANATIONS

usurous money-grabbing
bleak cold, exposed and desolate
where-e'er wherever
mind thoughts and feelings
appall shock

1. A rhetorical question is one where the expected answer is clear from the question. So, when Blake starts by asking 'Is this a holy thing?' it is obvious that the answer is 'No'. Find another rhetorical question in this poem and say what answer you think Blake expects.

2. Blake often uses a contrast to make his point. Re-read the first stanza. Which of the following are being contrasted in the first stanza?

   warmth and cold *wealth and poverty* *holiness and wickedness*

   Explain your choice.

3. The third stanza gives four images of life in the charity school.

   a List the four images.

   b Explain what each image suggests to you, for example:

   'the sun never shining' gives an impression of a dark world without the promise of a new day.

4. Here are four thoughts about this poem.
   - There's nothing 'holy' about the way children are treated here.
   - When Blake says 'It is a land of poverty', he doesn't mean it.
   - The last stanza is about what happens somewhere normal.
   - Children are still poor and hungry in rich countries.

   a Write out the one that you think captures most effectively what Blake is saying in this poem. Say why you chose it.

   b Share your ideas as a group or a class. How far do you agree?

5. Write a paragraph about how Blake tries to convince his readers that the treatment of poor children is wrong. You could look at:
   - the images of life in a charity school
   - the contrasts in the first stanza
   - the use of rhetorical questions.

Check your learning

- Choose two sentences from your answers that sum up for you what William Blake wanted to say in this poem.
- Read your sentences to each other.
- Talk about whether you think poems like this made Blake popular or not.

Learning extra

Choose a subject that you feel strongly about, e.g. not being treated equally, age prejudice, eating meat, being compared to others, parents' expectations. Write about it for a teenage magazine. Use questions, as Blake does, to point out the madness of the situation you are describing.

London

WILLIAM BLAKE

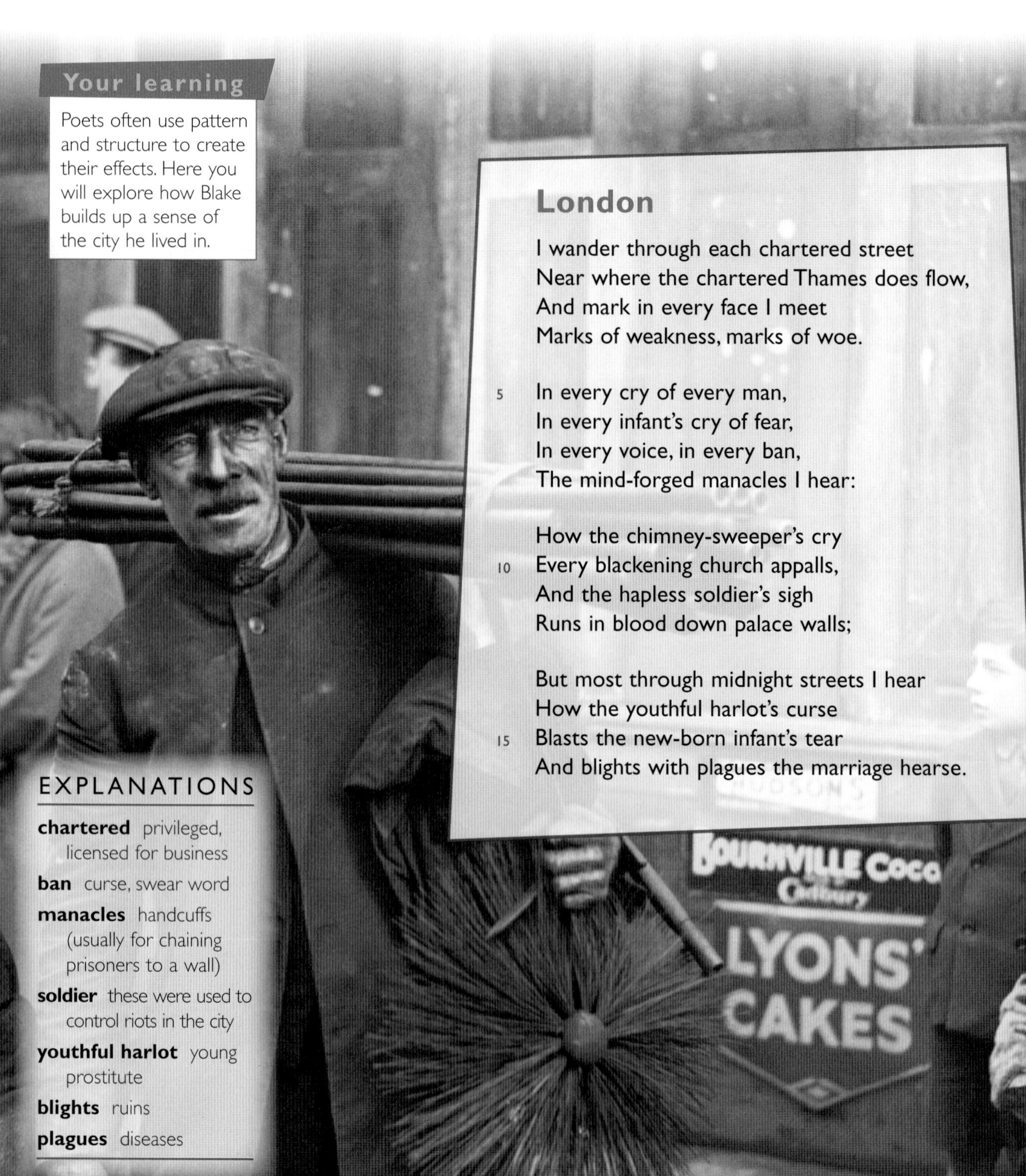

Your learning

Poets often use pattern and structure to create their effects. Here you will explore how Blake builds up a sense of the city he lived in.

London

I wander through each chartered street
Near where the chartered Thames does flow,
And mark in every face I meet
Marks of weakness, marks of woe.

5 In every cry of every man,
In every infant's cry of fear,
In every voice, in every ban,
The mind-forged manacles I hear:

How the chimney-sweeper's cry
10 Every blackening church appalls,
And the hapless soldier's sigh
Runs in blood down palace walls;

But most through midnight streets I hear
How the youthful harlot's curse
15 Blasts the new-born infant's tear
And blights with plagues the marriage hearse.

EXPLANATIONS

chartered privileged, licensed for business

ban curse, swear word

manacles handcuffs (usually for chaining prisoners to a wall)

soldier these were used to control riots in the city

youthful harlot young prostitute

blights ruins

plagues diseases

1 Look at these words from the poem:

woe (line 4) *appalls* (line 10) *hapless* (line 11) *hearse* (line 16)

a Use a dictionary to find out what they mean.

b Look at the lines the words came from, and discuss what these lines mean.

2 Repetition can be used to make a point stand out more. Look at the second stanza.

a Which important word is repeated five times?

b What effect does its repetition have on your understanding of the poem?

c Replace it with another word like 'the' or 'a'. What difference does this make?

3 Like many poets, Blake uses imagery in his poetry. Imagery is a collection of images. Images are words/phrases that writers use to help create pictures in our minds. Here are several images from the poem:

- mind-forged manacles
- How the chimney-sweeper's cry/Every blackening church appalls
- the hapless soldier's sigh/Runs in blood down palace walls
- the marriage hearse.

Explain what these images mean to you, for example:

'mind-forged manacles' sound like chains that are created in someone's head rather than made of steel.

4 **a** What impression does Blake give you of London? Is it cheerful, sad, miserable, dangerous, dark, happy, deadly, dirty, desperate? Suggest any other ideas of your own.

b Write two paragraphs about how the poet builds up a picture of London across the four stanzas. You should write about Blake's use of repetition and imagery as well as ideas of your own.

Check your learning

Complete these sentences:

- William Blake does more than just describe London, he...
- The most effective way in which he does this is...

Compare your answers and talk about how Blake felt about the city in which he lived.

Learning extra

Think about a city today. What would you notice as you walked through it? Write a description of a modern city in 50 words. Try to focus on particular details as Blake does, but build up the piece in a way that suits your style of writing.

Linking the William Blake poems

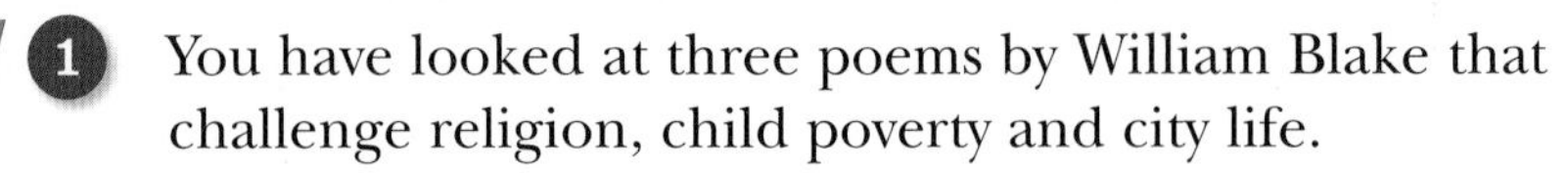

Your learning

'Artist or genius … mystic or madman? Probably he is all.' This was the opinion of someone who actually met William Blake. In the three poems in this section, Blake asks people to look and think again. Here you will consider the different ways these poems challenged people and comment on their effects.

1 You have looked at three poems by William Blake that challenge religion, child poverty and city life.

a Which poem is described by each of these statements?

- It's about walking through a city…
- It's a series of questions…
- It's a complaint about poverty…

b Copy out each of the statements listed above. Add words of your own to give each statement more detail.

2 Read the three statements below about each poem.

a Which statement best describes how you see the poem?

b Write the statement out and add your own comment about the effect that the poem creates.

'The Tyger'

- *This isn't about a tiger at all, it's about being afraid of God.*
- *Blake is fascinated by the thought that God can create both the gentle and the terrifying.*
- *It's a kind of nightmare vision of the evil powers that are out there in the world.*

'Holy Thursday'

- *It's a question and answer poem. He is asking whether the level of poverty he sees can be right and the answer is obviously 'no'.*
- *Blake tries to make you feel sorry for the children, but in a very sentimental way.*
- *Imagine a long procession of poor, ragged children. They are being dragged along to a grand church service to make rich people feel good. This is what makes Blake angry.*

'London'

- *It's the 1794 equivalent of a TV documentary. Blake's eyes and ears scan the streets and he picks out the very worst of London life.*
- *It's a vivid picture, but exaggerated. The idea that 'every' voice is calling out makes Blake sound more like a preacher than a poet.*
- *Contrast makes this poem work. It starts with business and trade but soon turns to the human costs of city life.*

3. Which poem do you think is most likely to anger or offend adults? To help you answer this, read the following opinions to help you get started:
   - '"The Tyger" because people like their religion simple and comfortable.'
   - '"Holy Thursday". You don't want to be giving money to charity just to have some poet tell you that it is nowhere near enough.'
   - '"London" as it's telling people that their whole city lifestyle is false and a scandal.'

4. **a** Write down one positive detail – a strong idea or powerful line – from each poem.

   b Write down one thing you are not sure about for each poem.

   c In groups or as a class, collect together the positive points and the questions.

	Positive points	Questions
The Tyger		
Holy Thursday		
London		

5. William Blake was an artist as well as a poet. Imagine you are instructing an artist to illustrate three of Blake's images. Describe three images that Blake includes in any of the three poems, giving as much detail as you can.

6. William Blake is a poet who people remember and feel strongly about. Write three paragraphs explaining why this is the case. Use points and examples from your work on earlier questions here, as well as your own ideas. You could comment on:
   - his use of descriptive language and imagery
   - how he brings places and characters to life
   - the strength of his opinions on issues important to him.

Check your learning

Write down what you think is:
- the most effective way that Blake challenges society in these poems
- the image or description that had most impact on you.

Share your answers with a partner.
From the work you have been doing on these three poems, talk about and agree on one question you would like to ask William Blake.

Learning extra

How would you want to challenge the leaders of our society as Blake did in his time? What would it be about – *poverty … waste … the environment … recycling … rights … elections … war … homelessness?* Write a newspaper advertisement to get people to share your interest.

Your eyes have over two million working parts and will process over twenty million images of the world for you during your life. This section takes three poems, all written in the first person, and explores what they describe.

Your learning

A poet can look at a subject like the effect of divorce on children differently from the way a newspaper or other forms of writing might. Here you will explore how this subject is presented in a poem.

Weekend visit

ALAN SMITH

Weekend visit

Hello there, Dad.
It's OK that you're late.
I know you had a date with her,
and she resents
5 these Saturdays.
Sometimes, you know, I do as well.
What's that? 'So, what today?'
You ask, with that forced smile.
Should I have laughed?
10 You want me to, I think.
I really feel a fool.
Sometimes, somehow
it only makes it worse
than if you never
15 came around at all.
The movies? Fine.
It doesn't matter
I've seen it before.
But I'll be with you, in the dark.
20 You won't see if I'm crying (though I won't!)
And you can hide
that you are thinking of your new love.
And I can keep the knowledge secret
that I'm numb inside.

25 You're smiling at me now,
That booming laugh, you try so hard.
What's that, Dad? Did you speak?
I was a million miles away.
Back in the days
30 when you and I and Mum
picnicked by the lake, or when
you took me to the park,
back in the days before things crashed
back in the years
35 before things went so dark.

EXPLANATIONS

resent feel angry or bitter about something

1. Look at the first stanza (lines 1–15). What is the situation like between the child and the father at the beginning of the weekend visit?

2. Look at the second and third stanzas (lines 16–36). Find two pieces of evidence in these lines that the weekend visit is not getting better as it goes on. Give an explanation for the words/lines that you choose, e.g. *'you try so hard' – the fact that the dad is having to make such an effort makes it sound as if the whole thing is unnatural and forced, as if he knows it isn't working.*

3. Emotions in poetry are created in a number of ways. Sometimes they are obvious from the poet's language. Sometimes they are more hidden.

   a In pairs, find examples of emotions that are clear in the poem.

   b Now find examples of emotions that are hidden or implicit in the poem. You will need to refer to the words that suggest them.

4. **a** Read the following list of different kinds of information about divorce:

   - statistics
   - information about trends
   - personal stories
   - court cases
   - feelings
   - comments by experts
   - a sense of what the experience is like

   For each kind of information, decide whether you would expect to find it in a poem, a newspaper article or both.

   b Now list at least three reasons why newspaper articles and poems are different. Think about the different kinds of content, and ways of expressing it, that poems and newspaper articles use.
   Reason 1 could be:

   1 *Newspaper articles are more likely to be focusing on facts.*

5. Write two paragraphs about how the poet makes you feel about the situation between the child and the father.
   You could write about:

   - not knowing what to say or do in this kind of situation
   - hiding feelings and feeling uncomfortable
   - dreaming of the past.

Check your learning

- What are the most important things you explored in this poem that you would not expect to find in a newspaper?
- Complete the sentence: 'A poem can show you…'
- Compare your answers with a partner's.

Learning extra

'Weekend visit' tells you what the narrator is thinking more than what s/he is saying. Try writing a piece where you are addressing a parent or teacher but you are saying most of the things in your head out loud. It could be about homework, or the time you're expected to be home, or any regular problem.

Grandfather

SUSAN HRYNKOW

Your learning

It is not only what poets say that matters, it is how they say it. Here you will look carefully at the words and phrases that the poet chooses, in order to create a character and use what you learn to describe a character that you remember.

Grandfather

I remember
His sparse white hair and lean face…
Creased eyes that twinkled when he laughed
And the sea-worn skin
5 Patterned to a latticework of lines.
I remember
His blue-veined, calloused hands.
Long gnarled fingers
Stretching out towards the fire –
10 Three fingers missing –
Yet he was able to make model yachts
And weave baskets.
Each bronzed Autumn
He would gather berries
15 Each breathing Spring
His hands were filled with flowers.

I remember
Worshipping his fisherman's yarns.
Watching his absorbed expression
20 As he solved the daily crossword
With the slim cigarette, hand rolled,
Placed between his lips.
I remember
The snowdrops
25 The impersonal hospital bed.
The reek of antiseptic.

I remember, too,
The weeping child
And wilting daffodils
30 Laid upon his grave.

EXPLANATIONS

sparse thinly spread or scattered

latticework a criss-cross pattern

calloused hardened (of skin)

gnarled twisted with knotty swellings

reek stink

1. Re-read the first seven lines of the poem, and write down ten words from those lines that you think are important in describing what the poet's grandfather looked like.

   Choose two words/phrases and describe what they suggest to you.

2. The poet uses the words 'I remember' five times.

   a Copy and complete the table below to list the points where 'I remember' is used.

   b Find the lines in the poem that start with 'I remember' and cover these subjects:

Lines	Subject
	illness
	hands
	hearing and watching
	at the graveside
	face

3. Adjectives are a key part of descriptive writing, as they add more detail to a noun. For example, the grandfather's hair is described as 'white' and 'sparse'. In pairs, find and list at least three more adjectives in the poem. Discuss what they add to the poem.

4. The poet's choice of words and phrases brings the memory of the narrator's grandfather to life. Choose three separate phrases or lines from the poem, and explain how they help you to imagine the grandfather clearly and vividly. Here is one example:

   I like the description of the 'sparse white hair'. He isn't bald but there isn't much left to cover him, just like there isn't much time left in his life.

5. Write two paragraphs explaining how Susan Hrynkow builds up the picture of her grandfather, detail by detail. Look carefully at the order in which she describes things, and the effects of each of the three stanzas.

Check your learning

- Discuss in pairs what you have learnt about the use of description in this poem.
- Read each other's answers to question 4 and see what points you can add by pooling your ideas.

Learning extra

Write your own poem describing someone who has mattered in your life.

It can be anyone: they don't have to be old. Start each stanza with the words 'I remember'. Use words and phrases to help your reader picture this person in their mind.

Quieter Than Snow

Berlie Doherty

Your learning

Poets often use description to create atmosphere and to help the reader visualise a scene. Here, you will explore how the poet uses similes and appeals to the senses.

Quieter Than Snow

I went to school a day too soon
And couldn't understand
Why silence hung in the yard like sheets
Nothing to flap or spin, no creaks
5 Or shocks of voices, only air.

And the car park empty of teachers' cars
Only the first September leaves
Dropping like paper. No racks of bikes
No kicking legs, no fights,
10 No voices, laughter, anything.

Yet the door was open. My feet
Sucked down the corridor. My reflection
Walked with me past the hall.
My classroom smelt of nothing. And the silence
15 Rolled like thunder in my ears.

At every desk a still child stared at me
Teachers walked through walls and back again
Cupboard doors swung open, and out crept
More silent children, and still more.

20 They tiptoed round me
Touched me with ice-cold hands
And opened up their mouths with laughter
That was

Quieter than snow.

1 Berlie Doherty uses *similes* to help the reader picture what the school was like on that day before term. Similes compare one object with another, using 'like' or 'as'.

Copy out the phrases below and explain how each one gives you a sense of what the experience was like. The first one has been started for you.

a silence hung in the yard like sheets (line 3)

Silence is being compared to sheets that have been put out to dry on a washing line. Just as the sheets simply hang there…

b the first September leaves
Dropping like paper (lines 7–8)

c the silence
Rolled like thunder in my ears. (lines 14–15)

2 *Atmosphere* refers to the overall mood of a poem. This could suggest a variety of feelings. In this poem, atmosphere is created by description. What is unusual here is that the description is often about things that are missing.

a Find and list the places in the poem where the description is about what *isn't* there. You could start by looking for words like 'nothing' or 'no'.

b Look at your list. What is the effect of the poet describing missing things?

3 The poet also refers to the five senses (sight, sound, smell, touch and taste) several times.

a Find and list as many examples as you can of the five senses in the poem. For example, 'No voices' refers to sound.

b Why do you think the poet makes so many references to the senses?

4 Write five sentences about how the poet has made the scene in the school come to life through the description she has used. Comment on:

- the similes you have looked at
- the listing of things that are not there
- the way the poem appeals to the senses.

Check your learning

- Share the best of the five sentences you wrote about the poem. Say why you chose the sentence you did.
- What have you learnt from reading this poem that you can apply to your reading of another poem?

Learning extra

- Look at lines 16–24. What do you think is happening here?
- How could you bring this scene to life if you were filming it? Think about how to capture the atmosphere of the poem. You could do this as a storyboard.

Linking the *Through my eyes* poems

Your learning

The three poems you have studied are all written in the first person, but present their subjects in a variety of ways. Here you will look at what makes the poems distinctive and different, then experiment with different forms and styles yourself.

1. Read the poems again and decide which of the following descriptions best fits each poem:
   - an experience remembered from the past
   - one side of a dialogue
   - a memory of someone.

2. Poets use a variety of techniques in their poems. Which *Through my eyes* poems fit the following descriptions? (More than one poem may fit a description.)
   - The poem is mainly in the present tense.
   - The poem is mainly in the past tense.
   - The poem uses repetition.

3. This section has looked at poems in the first person, so now it is your turn to write a poem using 'I' rather than 'he' or 'she'. Your poem can be true to life, made up, or a mixture of the two. Good writing requires planning, so the following steps will take you through the planning process.

Step 1: Choose your subject

You can write about an experience or experiences at school, *or* about someone in your family *or* a close friend.

Make notes as quickly as you can about what you might want to say. Remember: you will be describing how things feel as well as what they look like.

Step 2: Plan your approach

Look at the boxes headed 'Style' and 'Tone'. Use the ideas in these boxes to help you decide on the approach you are going to take. Below are some of the questions you will need to consider in planning your poem.

- Is it going to be serious or humorous?
- Is it looking back or describing things as they happen?
- What is the narrator of the poem going to sound like?

Style

formal
informal
reflective
down-to-earth
light-hearted

Tone

troubled	friendly
loving	angry
puzzled	scared
hopeful	sad
desperate	unsure

Step 3: Decide on the form

The form of the poem means the type of poem, such as haiku or limerick. Using the 'Types of poetry' list opposite, decide what form you want your poem to take. When deciding on the form of the poem, think about:

- The form you choose should suit the subject matter and tone. For example: if you want to write a serious poem you probably wouldn't choose to write a limerick; if you wanted to write a love poem you might choose to write a sonnet.

- How much do you want to write?
- You will have to keep to the rules of the form – will this suit your subject matter and style?

Step 4: Writing

As you start to write you will need to decide on the following:

- whether to write in stanzas
- what your line length is
- when to use punctuation
- whether to use descriptive language
- whether to appeal to the senses
- whether to use rhyme, repetition, imagery and sound patterns.

Now have a go at the first draft of your poem.

4 Read through your first draft with a partner, then re-draft your poem. Use the following checklist and your ideas to make any necessary revisions to your poem.

- Is it in the first person throughout?
- Do the style and tone you have chosen suit your poem's content?
- Have you kept to the rules of the form throughout?
- Does the form you have chosen suit your poem's content?

Types of poetry

acrostic
cinquain
dialogue
free verse
haiku
limerick
shape
monologue
narrative
rap
sonnet
tanka

Check your learning

- Listen in groups to what other people have written.
- Discuss what is good about each poem and why these features are 'good'.
- What could be improved?
- What are your strengths and weaknesses?

Learning extra

Try other approaches to your subject. If you've written a short poem such as a tanka, try writing something longer. If you've written a descriptive poem, try dealing with your subject in dialogue form. It's your choice, but take the opportunity to try things out. What works best for you?

When you compare poems you consider the similarities and differences between them. These may be to do with content, form, structure and/or the ways the poets use words. In this section you will look at two pairs of poems. In each pair, the first poem was written some time before the second one.

He Wishes for the Cloths of Heaven

W.B. Yeats

Your learning

Sometimes we can see similarities between poems even though they are written by different people and are about different things. Here you will explore the ways in which these poems are similar.

EXPLANATIONS

Enwrought an archaic word meaning decorated

He Wishes for the Cloths of Heaven

Had I the heavens' embroidered cloths,
Enwrought with golden and silver light,
The blue and the dim and the dark cloths
Of night and light and the half-light,
5 I would spread the cloths under your feet:
But I, being poor, have only my dreams;
I have spread my dreams under your feet;
Tread softly because you tread on my dreams.

The Boy with a Cloud in his Hand

Sheenagh Pugh

The Boy with a Cloud in his Hand

He hasn't got much: not a roof,
nor a job, nor any great hopes,
but he's got a cloud in his hand
and he thinks he might squeeze
5 till the rain falls over the town,
and he thinks he might tease
the cottonwool fluff into strands
of thin mist, and blank everything out,
and he thinks he might blow
10 this dandelion clock so high,
it will never come down, and he thinks
he might eat it, a taste of marshmallow
sliding inside him, filling him up
with emptiness, till he's all space,
15 and he thinks, when he's hollow and full,
he might float away.

1 With a partner, talk about the things you have worked out about each of these poems. Draw a spider diagram for each poem, to record your ideas.

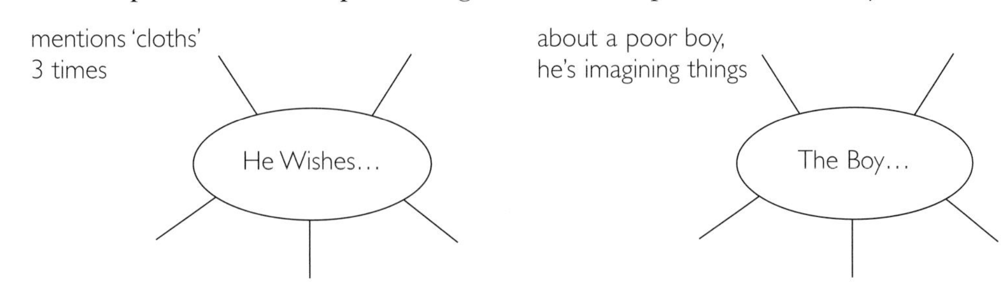

2 Look again at 'He Wishes for the Cloths of Heaven'. Did you work out that the *Cloths of Heaven* refers to the sky?

a What adjectives does Yeats use in the first three lines of the poem to describe the sky? What kind of picture of the sky do these adjectives create? What would he like to do with these cloths?

3 Look again at 'The Boy with a Cloud in his Hand'. The cloud seems to represent his imagination and the things he would like to do.

a What different things does he think of doing?

b What verbs are used to describe what the boy *thinks he might* do? Choose two of these verbs. Explain what each one suggests to you.

4 Look again at the last two lines of each poem.

a How does each ending make you feel?

b Talk about how good you think they are as endings, which one you like best and the reasons for your preference.

Learning extra

Write a paragraph or a poem describing what you dream of.

Check your learning

a Copy out the comparison below, and use your knowledge of the poems, and the word bank below, to help you fill in the spaces.

Both the man in the first poem and the boy in the second poem are _____. They both _____. The man dreams of giving his lady the _____. The boy dreams of having a _____ in his hand and eventually _____ away like a cloud. Both writers choose words that help the _____ picture what they are describing. In the first poem the writer uses _____ such as *embroidered* and _____ to describe the _____. The writer of the second poem uses _____ such as tease and _____ to describe what the boy might do.

cloud	blank	poor	floating	adjectives	dream
golden	cloths of heaven	verbs	reader	sky	

b Copy and complete this final part of the comparison without a word bank:

I had different feelings about the two poems. The first poem made me feel _________ because _____. The second poem made me feel _____ because _________. Of the two poems, I preferred _____. The reasons for this are _________.

Sonnet 18

William Shakespeare

Your learning

When you read these two sonnets you will notice similarities and differences between them. Here you will explore the sonnet form and learn about parody. You will also develop your skills in comparing two poems.

Sonnet 18

Shall I compare thee to a summer's day?
Thou art more lovely and more temperate:
Rough winds do shake the darling buds of May,
And summer's lease hath all too short a date:
5 Sometime too hot the eye of Heaven shines,
And often is his gold complexion dimm'd:
And every fair from fair sometime declines,
By chance, or nature's changing course, untrimm'd.
But thy eternal summer shall not fade
10 Nor lose possession of that fair thou ow'st;
Nor shall Death brag thou wander'st in his shade,
When in eternal lines to time thou grow'st;
So long as men can breathe, or eyes can see,
So long lives this, and this gives life to thee.

EXPLANATIONS

temperate mild
summer's lease the length of summer
eye of heaven the sun
his gold complexion the sun's rays
untrimm'd unchecked
ow'st short for 'ownst' meaning 'own'

Shakespeare's 18th Worm

CELIA WARREN

Shakespeare's 18th Worm

Shall I compare thee to a bit of string?
Thou art more bristly and more flexible.
Rough soils do hold the horrid stones that sting
And cruel clay is heavily inedible.

5 Sometime too wet the mouth of heaven spits,
And often are the segments clogged with dirt,
And every squirm from squirm sometime desists,
By chance of nature's sending in a bird.

But thy eternal wriggle shan't grow weak,
10 Nor lose possession of that squirm thou hast,
Nor blackbird brag thou danglest from his beak,
When in eternal stringiness thou growest.

So long as worms can squirm or hedgehogs fast,
So long as birds are late your life will last.

EXPLANATIONS

inedible cannot be eaten

1. *Sonnet* means 'little song'. A Shakespearean sonnet has certain features. See if you can work out what some of these are by:
   - counting the number of lines in the poem
   - working out the rhyme scheme
   - counting the number of syllables, or beats, in each line.

   Using what you have worked out, list three rules for writing a Shakespearean sonnet.

2. Answer these questions to help you understand 'Sonnet 18':

   a Who do you think the *thee* (you) in the first line is?

   b List at least three different things you think of when you picture a summer's day.

   c Re-read lines 3–8. What criticisms does Shakespeare make of summer?

   d Re-read lines 9–12. Explain the promise Shakespeare makes in these lines.

   e What does Shakespeare suggest about the power of poetry in lines 13–14?

3. Tell a partner what you think 'Sonnet 18' has to say about love and poetry. Listen to their opinions. Share your joint thoughts with another pair and make notes on your discussion.

4. Sometimes a writer will mimic the style of another writer in a humorous way. This is called *parody*. 'Shakespeare's 18th Worm' is a parody of 'Sonnet 18'. Working with a partner, spot and list the ways in which 'Shakespeare's 18th Worm' is similar to 'Sonnet 18'. You should think about its meaning and the way it is written.

5. Identify the words used in 'Shakespeare's 18th Worm' that are identical to 'Sonnet 18'. You could do this by copying out 'Shakespeare's 18th Worm' and underlining or highlighting the identical words.

   Shall I compare thee to a bit of string?
   Thou art more bristly and more flexible.

6 Copy and complete the table below to record the similarities and differences between 'Shakespeare's 18th Worm' and 'Sonnet 18'.

Features	Sonnet 18	Shakespeare's 18th Worm
Number of lines		
Rhyme scheme		
Number of syllables in each line		
Number of stanzas		
Who/what it is written to		
What it compares the person/thing to		
Its tone		
First line		
Last line		

7 Write a comparison of 'Sonnet 18' and 'Shakespeare's 18th Worm'. Using your learning so far, follow these four steps.

Step 1 Write an opening paragraph and mention:

- the similarities in the titles
- the similarities in number of lines, the rhyme schemes and the number of syllables in each line
- the differences in the stanza forms.

Step 2 Write a second paragraph and say something about:

- the differences in the subjects of the poems
- the differences in what is said about the subjects.

Step 3 Write a third paragraph in which you point out:

- which poem is a parody of the other
- the differences in tone
- the ways one poem imitates the other by using the same words.

Step 4 Write a final paragraph in which you:

- state which poem you like best
- explain the reasons for your choice.

Check your learning

Check carefully that you have written about all of the bullet points in Steps 1 to 4. If you have missed anything out, or have anything else you want to say, make extra notes at the end of your writing.

Information

Tone

The tone of a poem describes the poet's voice, which might be serious, funny and so on.

Learning extra

Write your own sonnet, beginning 'Shall I compare thee to…'. You could write it for:

- someone you know
- an animal
- a pebble on a beach
- a plant
- a computer
- a monster
- something else.

Remember that your sonnet should have:

- 14 lines
- an *ababcdcdefefgg* rhyme scheme
- ten syllables in each line.

You can use words directly from Shakespeare's poem, as Celia Warren did.

Thomas Hardy was a poet and novelist, and many of his stories are still being read and made into films today. His first volume of poetry was published when he was 58, and he continued to write poetry until his death in 1928.

A Light Snow-Fall after Frost

THOMAS HARDY

Your learning

Sometimes poets take an everyday scene and, through description, enable the reader to see it clearly. Here you will examine closely some of the words Hardy chooses to describe one such scene.

A Light Snow-Fall after Frost

On the flat road a man at last appears:
    How much his whitening hairs
Owe to the settling snow's mute anchorage,
And how much to life's rough pilgrimage,
5   One cannot certify.

    The frost is on the wane,
And cobwebs hanging close outside the pane
Pose as festoons of thick white worsted there,
Of their pale presence no eye being aware
10   Till the rime made them plain.

    A second man comes by;
His ruddy beard brings fire to the pallid scene:
    His coat is faded green;
    Hence seems that his mien
15   Wears something of the dye
Of the berried holm-trees that he passes nigh.

The snow-feathers so gently swoop that though
    But a half an hour ago
The road was brown, and now is starkly white,
20 A watcher would have failed defining quite
    When it transformed so.

EXPLANATIONS

certify say for certain
pilgrimage journey
ruddy red
mute silent
festoons decorative chains
worsted wool
rime frost
pallid pale, lacking colour
mien appearance
holm-trees holly trees
nigh near

1 List the different things described in the poem.

2 **a** Poets often say a great deal in just a few words. Think about the phrase *the settling snow's mute anchorage.* Does it suggest that:

- the snow is melting
- the snow falls silently
- the snow is lying
- the snow is soft
- the snow is determined
- the snow is still falling
- the snow has a grip on everything
- the snow is heavy
- it has stopped snowing
- the snow is light?

b Poets choose their words carefully. With a partner, talk about why Thomas Hardy used the following words:

- *settling* instead of *falling*
- *mute* instead of *silent*
- *anchorage* instead of *grip.*

c What is uncertain about the man's appearance?

3 Thomas Hardy uses a simile to compare the cobwebs to *festoons of thick white worsted.* A simile is a comparison using 'like' or 'as'.

a List at least three things that this simile suggests about the cobwebs.

b The poet also says the cobwebs *pose.* What does this verb suggest?

4 The third stanza describes a second man. Explain how his appearance is:

a contrasted with the scene around him

b compared with the scene around him.

5 An oxymoron is the joining of words with apparently opposing meanings. The poet tells us that *The snow-feathers so gently swoop.* Explain:

a how *gently* and *swoop* have opposing meanings

b what is suggested by the use of these two words together.

Check your learning

Now read the opening lines from another poem by Hardy:

I leant upon a coppice gate *coppice: small group of trees*
When Frost was spectre-gray,
And Winter's dregs made desolate
The weakening eye of day. (from 'The Darkling Thrush')

a Write three questions about the poet's word choices. Write the answers and keep them separate from the questions.

b Swap your questions with a partner for him/her to answer.

c Check your partner's answers against the ones you wrote and talk about any differences between them.

Learning extra

The final stanza refers to a *watcher.* Re-read the whole poem. What clues tell you who the watcher is, how long he has been watching and where he is watching from?

Heredity

THOMAS HARDY

Your learning

Poets sometimes present an unusual idea or make us think about something in a different way. Here you will consider the idea explored in the poem and your own response to this.

Heredity

I am the family face;
Flesh perishes, I live on,
Projecting trait and trace
Through time to times anon,
5 And leaping from place to place
Over oblivion.

The years-heired feature that can
In curve and voice and eye
Despise the human span
10 Of durance – that is I;
The eternal thing in man,
That heeds no call to die.

EXPLANATIONS

heredity the passing on of characteristics from parents to children through the genes

trait and trace characteristic features that distinguish a particular person

years-heired feature characteristic passed on genetically through the years

durance imprisonment

1 Jot down your own ideas on what death is, whether you believe in life after death and, if so, what form it takes. Here are some different ideas to start you thinking:

When you die, you die.

People have souls that live on after death.

The body dies but the spirit lives.

One person lives many lives.

You live on through your children.

It is possible to speak with the dead.

2 In groups of three or four, talk about death and the possibility of life after death. Aim to express your ideas clearly and to explain why you think as you do. Use examples to help you, where relevant. Make sure you consider:

- what you think death is
- whether you believe in life after death and your reasons
- what you would say to someone whose ideas are different from yours.

Make a note of any points that you change your mind about.

3 With a partner, or in your group, re-read 'Heredity'. Answer these questions to help you understand the poem.

a. What is the *family face*?

b How does it live on when *flesh perishes*?

c How might it leap *from place to place*?

d What do you think Hardy is saying about life when he describes it as the human *span of durance*?

e In what way is the family face the *eternal thing in man*?

f How far do you agree with Hardy's ideas about heredity?

4 Suggest two reasons why Hardy wrote this poem in the first person.

Check your learning

Write three paragraphs.
In the first, explain Hardy's ideas on heredity as shown in this poem, using quotations where relevant.
In the second, explain your response to Hardy's ideas and the way he has expressed them.
In the third, comment on whether your personal ideas on death and life after death have influenced, or been influenced by, your reading of the poem.

Learning extra

Make a group or class collection of different beliefs about death and life after death. You could also include a copy of Hardy's poem.

The Walk

THOMAS HARDY

Your learning

Sometimes you will be asked to write a detailed answer to a general question on a poem. Here you will learn what details you need to include in your answer.

The Walk

You did not walk with me
Of late to the hill-top tree
By the gated ways,
As in earlier days;
5 You were weak and lame,
So you never came,
And I went alone, and I did not mind,
Not thinking of you as left behind.

I walked up there to-day
10 Just in the former way;
Surveyed around
The familiar ground
By myself again:
What difference, then?
15 Only that underlying sense
Of the look of a room on returning thence.

EXPLANATIONS

surveyed had a look

Hardy's wife of forty years died shortly before he wrote this poem.

Work with a partner and keep notes on your answers to questions 1–5.

1 Show that you understand the meaning of the poem. Work out:

- to whom the poem is written
- what Hardy is remembering
- his past and present feelings
- why he feels this way now.

2 Show that you understand how Hardy organises his ideas. Say how he:

- separates the past from the present
- uses different line lengths.
- uses rhyme

3 Comment on the way Hardy uses words. Think about:

- why he uses simple words and a simple rhyme scheme
- how he creates a sense of being alone throughout the poem
- the effect of using the first person throughout.

4 Use evidence from the poem to support your comments. You can:

- refer to details in a poem without quoting directly from it, for example:
  The poet writes about how he and his wife used to go walking.
- quote words and phrases directly from a poem, for example:
  In later years she could not go because she was 'weak and lame'.
- quote whole lines from a poem, for example:
  He questions what is different between the past and the present and there is sadness when he says it is:
  'Only the underlying sense
  Of the look of a room on returning thence.'

5 Develop your comment, for example: *We learn that in later years she could not go because she was 'weak and lame'. These words show his wife's helplessness and suggest that she would have gone had she been able to.*
Write a comment on the third example in question 4.

6 Write three comments that show your personal response to what the poem is about, the way it is written and how it makes you feel.

7 Using your notes to help you, answer the question: **What** ideas does Hardy express and **how** does he express them in 'The Walk'?

Check your learning

Swap your answer to question 7 with a partner. Tick where your partner has:

- shown understanding of the ideas and how they are organised
- discussed the way Hardy uses words
- used evidence from the poem
- developed their comments
- explained their personal response.

Learning extra

Answer one of the following questions:

- **What** does Hardy describe and **how** does he describe it in 'A Light Snow-Fall'?
- **What** idea does Hardy develop in 'Heredity' and **how** does he develop it?

Linking the Thomas Hardy poems

Your learning

Here you will look again at the three poems by Thomas Hardy on pages 78–82. You will explore:

- the way the language reflects the time in which the poems were written
- the relevance of the ideas to today's reader
- the variation in rhyme schemes
- what you learn about the poet from the poems
- how to explain your personal preference.

1 Hardy wrote these poems about 100 years ago. While his language is more familiar to us than Shakespeare's, there are some words that we would be unlikely to use in the same way today, for example: *Of the berried holm-trees that he passes nigh* ('A Light Snow-Fall after Frost').

a Explain what is different or unusual about this phrase.

b Make a list of words and phrases that show that Hardy's poetry was written a long time ago. For each item on your list, identify whether it is the words themselves that are unusual, or the way they are used.

2 Even if the language is unfamiliar, the content can still be relevant today.

a Say what each poem is about and how relevant it is to a modern reader.

b Might a poet write about similar things today? Explain your answer.

3 Rhyme is the repetition of sounds from word to word or from line to line. A rhyme occurs when two or more words have matching sounds. When rhyme occurs at the close of lines it is called end rhyme.

To describe the pattern of end rhyme – called the rhyme scheme – we use a simple system: lines with the same end rhyme are given the same letter, so the first rhyme is given the letter a, the second rhyme the letter b and so on. Hardy uses end rhyme in all three of these poems, for example:

You did not walk with me	a
Of late to the hill-top tree	a
By the gated ways,	b
As in earlier days;	b
You were weak and lame,	c

The full rhyme scheme for 'The Walk' is a-a-b-b-c-c-d-d e-e-f-f-g-g-h-h.

a Work out and write down the rhyme schemes for 'Heredity' and 'A Light Snow-Fall after Frost'.

b With a partner, suggest:

- two reasons why Hardy used a regular rhyme scheme for 'Heredity'
- two reasons why Hardy used an irregular rhyme scheme for 'A Light Snow-Fall after Frost'.

4 Poems often reveal things about their writer. Copy the table below. To complete your table, find evidence from any of the three poems that supports or contradicts the statements below. Your evidence does not have to be a quotation.

Statement	Agree/disagree	Evidence
Hardy observed nature closely.		
Hardy loved the countryside.		
Hardy did not believe in life after death.		
Hardy believed people live on through their descendants.		
Hardy enjoyed walking in the countryside.		
Hardy had a gloomy outlook on life.	*Not sure*	*'the human span of durance'* but seems to love nature
Hardy was lonely after his wife's death.		
Hardy did not love his wife when she was alive.		

5 Your personal response to a poem may be affected by your own experiences. For example, if snow is common where you live, you will find it easier to picture the scene in 'A Light Snow-Fall after Frost'. If you have just lost someone you loved, 'The Walk' will affect you more strongly.

It's not always a question of whether you 'like' a poem or not. It might be:

- what a poem makes you think about
- how it makes you feel
- your appreciation of the poet's craft.

Write a paragraph describing and explaining your response to each of the three poems. Use the bullet points above to help you organise your ideas and remember to refer to details in the poems.

Check your learning

In groups of three or four, read each others' personal responses. Draw a table to record your group's most- and least-liked poem and why you like/dislike it. Compare your table with another group's and discuss the reasons for any similarities or differences.

Learning extra

Sometimes knowing more about a poet's life helps you to understand their poetry better. Use the Internet and your library to find out more about Hardy's life and work. Make notes on your research.

'Read widely, poets and writers from different backgrounds, different cultures. Begin by writing about your own experiences. It's what you know best. Write about things that really matter to you, that excite you, so that at the end of the day at least you'd be writing about your own truth, and not somebody else's.' Grace Nichols giving advice to young writers.

On Receiving a Jamaican Postcard

GRACE NICHOLS

Your learning

As a reader of a poem you need to interpret the detail, using your own knowledge and opinions. You need to be sensitive to the tone of the poem. Here you will learn how to interpret the tone of the poem.

On Receiving a Jamaican Postcard

Colourful native entertainers
dancing at de edge of de sea
a man-an-woman combination
choreographing
5 de dream of de tourist industry

de two a dem in smiling conspiracy
to capture dis dream of de tourist industry

an de sea blue
an de sky blue
10 an de sand gold fuh true

an de sea blue
an de sky blue
an de sand gold fuh true

He staging a dance-prance
15 head in a red band
beating he waist drum
as if he want to drown she wid sound
an yes, he muscle looking strong

She a vision of frilly red
20 back-backing to he riddum
exposing she brown leg
arcing like lil mo
she will limbo into de sea

Anything fuh de sake of de tourist industry
25 Anything fuh de sake of de tourist industry

EXPLANATIONS

choreograph to compose the steps for a dance

1 The tourist industry is referred to four times in the poem. Discuss the statements below with a partner and say whether they are true, partly true or false. Give reasons for your decisions.

The tourist industry:

- improves the lives of local people
- always gives accurate information
- tells you everything you need to know about a place
- only tells you the good things about a place
- is good for the environment.

2 What do you think is meant by *de dream of de tourist industry*?

a Describe the scene pictured on the postcard.

b What kind of place does this scene convey to you?

c Describe the kind of holiday you would expect to have there.

3 The tone of a poem tells you the real attitude and intention of the speaker. In order to interpret tone, you need to think carefully about the poet's choice of words. What do the words *smiling conspiracy* suggest about the dancers and their attitude to what they are doing?

4 Re-read lines 14–23, the description of the dancers.

a Pick out and list the ways Grace Nichols makes them seem ridiculous.

b Look back at your answers to questions 3 and 4a. What is the poet's attitude to these dancers?

5 We can work out things about the poet's tone from her use of repetition.

a Look at the repeated stanza in the middle of the poem. Why do you think the poet decided to repeat these lines?

b Find another example of a repeated line. What do you think the poet is trying to draw to the reader's attention here?

c Would you describe the poet's tone as sarcastic, cynical, angry, optimistic, happy, or something else? Give your reasons for your choice.

Check your learning

On your own, write two questions to ask Grace Nichols about her attitude to the tourist industry, based on your work above. Next, in a group, imagine you are interviewing her. One group member is to take her role. In turn, put your questions to Grace Nichols. If she answers in a way that appears to contradict what she said in the poem, ask her to explain further.

Learning extra

As Grace Nichols was aware, tourism can create problems. Do some research on its effects in Jamaica and other parts of the Caribbean. Produce a leaflet on the good and bad things about tourism in the Caribbean.

Two Old Black Men on a Leicester Square Park Bench

GRACE NICHOLS

Your learning

Many poems are written in free verse, which is not constrained by fixed patterns of rhyme or rhythm. Here you will investigate how Grace Nichols achieves different effects through her use of free verse.

Two Old Black Men on a Leicester Square Park Bench

What do you dream of you
old black men sitting
on park benches staunchly
wrapped up in scarves
5 and coats of silence
eyes far away from the cold
grey and strutting
pigeon
ashy fingers trembling
10 (though it's said that the old
hardly ever feel the cold)

do you dream revolutions
you could have forged
or mourn
15 some sunfull woman you
might have known a
hibiscus flower
ghost memories of desire

O it's easy
20 to rainbow the past
after all the letters from
home spoke of hardships

and the sun was traded long ago

EXPLANATIONS

hibiscus flower a brightly coloured flower found in the Caribbean

home the Caribbean

1. In free verse the poet decides when to start and end the lines. This may be decided by the natural rhythm of the words and/or the wish to emphasise certain words. Grace Nichols could have organised the first five lines like this:

   What do you dream of
   you old black men
   sitting
   on park benches staunchly
   wrapped up in
   scarves and coats of
   silence

   a With a partner, identify the differences between these lines and Grace Nichols's lines. Think about how different words are emphasised and what effects this has.

   b Experiment with reworking lines 7–12 to create different effects.

2. In free verse, poets sometimes focus on certain words to link lines and ideas. Look at *old* and *cold* in the first verse. How are these words used as links within the verse? What are the effects of this?

3. In this poem the shift to a new verse marks a shift in focus.

   a Identify the focus of each distinct verse.

   b Why is the final line of the poem placed on its own? Can you identify the link between this line and the *old* and *cold* of the first verse?

4. There is very little punctuation in this poem. This forces the reader to read closely and also enables a wider range of interpretations. For example, *staunchly* may refer to the way the old men are sitting, or to the way they are wrapped up, or both.

   Write down the words in the second verse whose meanings are not clear because of the absence of punctuation.

5. Look at the poem again. The verses decrease in length as the poem progresses. What might Grace Nichols be suggesting about:

   a the amount of sun in these old men's lives

   b the time they have yet to live?

Check your learning

Write a poem in free verse, about a person or people on a park bench. You could use Grace Nichols's opening line as a starting point. Show your poem to two or three other students. Think carefully about what they say before redrafting.

Learning extra

Imagine you are one of the old men in the poem who left the Caribbean many years ago to live in England. Write a letter to Grace Nichols, telling her about your life and your thoughts now you are old.

For Forest

GRACE NICHOLS

Your learning

Grace Nichols was born in Guyana, a country full of wild, unexplored forests. In this poem she uses imagery to make the forest seem like a living creature. This is called personification. Here you will explore the images she uses and their effects.

For Forest

Forest could keep secrets
Forest could keep secrets

Forest tune in everyday
to watersound and birdsound
5 Forest letting her hair down
to the teeming creeping of her forest-ground

But Forest don't broadcast her business
no Forest cover her business down
from sky and fast-eye sun
10 and when night come
and darkness wrap her like a gown
Forest is a bad dream woman

Forest dreaming about mountain
and when earth was young
15 Forest dreaming of the caress of gold
Forest rootsing with mysterious eldorado

and when howler monkey
wake her up with howl
Forest just stretch and stir
20 to a new day of sound

but coming back to secrets
Forest could keep secrets
Forest could keep secrets
And we must keep Forest

EXPLANATIONS

Eldorado a mythical city in South America, rich in treasure

1 We are told many things in 'For Forest'. Copy and complete the table below.

Quotation	Explanation
Forest could keep secrets	There may be things we don't know about in the forest
	The forest is full of different sounds
	The tangles and creepers are the forest's hair
But Forest don't broadcast her business no Forest cover her business down	
	The forest at night is the kind of place people have bad dreams about
	The forest has been there for a very long time
	She is like a famous mythical city rich in treasure
Forest just stretch and stir	

2 It is important to examine images closely and to be able to write about their effects in detail. Read the image below and the comment on it.

But Forest don't broadcast her business
no Forest cover her business down
from sky and fast-eye sun

In line 3 Nichols describes the forest 'tuning in', as though to TV or radio. This image is continued with the word 'broadcast'. The poem shows that, although Forest is aware of what is going on around 'her', 'she' is also a private person. 'Cover her business down' reminds the reader of the forest's canopy and secret nature. The forest is protected from outsiders such as the sky; even the 'fast-eye sun' cannot see what is going on.

Work in pairs; one of you should write about image A and one about image B, then swap and add your comments to your partner's.

A *and when night come*
And darkness wrap her like a gown
Forest is a bad dream woman

B *Forest dreaming of the caress of gold*
Forest rootsing with mysterious eldorado

Check your learning

Look at the range of images Nichols uses to present the forest to the reader.

a Suggest three reasons why she presents the forest as a woman.
b Say what kind of woman the forest could be. Explain why you think this.

Learning extra

Choose two more images from the poem; comment on each one in detail.

Linking the Grace Nichols poems

Your learning

Here you will look again at the three Grace Nichols poems on pages 86–90. You will explore her unusual uses of words, the things she reveals about Caribbean culture and the ways she uses rhyme and sound patterns to give structure to her poems.

1 Grace Nichols uses words in unusual ways, sometimes making completely new ones. For example, in 'On Receiving a Jamaican Postcard' she describes the male dancer as *staging a dance-prance*. She combines two rhyming words to create a humorous picture of the dance.

Look at the phrases below. Say why the highlighted words are unusual and comment on their effect.

a back-backing to he riddum
b some sunfull woman
c it's easy to rainbow the past
d to watersound and birdsound
e from sky and fast-eye sun
f Forest rootsing with the mysterious eldorado

2 Grace Nichols grew up in a village on the coast of Guyana, in the Caribbean; her roots influence many of her poems.

Look again at 'On Receiving a Jamaican Postcard' and 'Two Old Black Men on a Leicester Square Park Bench'. List the things they tell you about the Caribbean and its people.

3 The language of Nichols's poetry combines standard English with Creole, a language spoken in the West Indies, and is designed to capture the rhythms and sounds of speech.

a Look again at 'On Receiving a Jamaican Postcard'. Copy the list of language features below, and note down examples of each one.

- alternative pronunciation shown by different consonants, e.g. *d* instead of *th*
- different pronouns, e.g. *he* instead of *his*
- words being shortened
- hyphen showing two words almost pronounced as one
- words written as they are pronounced
- verbs missed out.

b Compare your answers with a partner's. Change or add to your notes after discussion if you need to.

4 All three poems are written in free verse, with no fixed patterns of rhyme or rhythm. Rhyme is, nevertheless, evident in all of them. Rhyme has nothing to do with spelling: English is full of words that have similar spelling but different sounds, e.g. *crow, cow*. Rhyme has to do with sounds; in order to hear it, you need to read the poetry aloud.

There are different ways of using rhyme in poetry:

a End rhyme occurs at the ends of lines. Write down examples of end rhyme from 'On Receiving a Jamaican Postcard' and 'For Forest'.

b Internal rhyme occurs within or between lines, e.g. *head in a red band.* Look through the poems, and find and write down at least two other examples of internal rhyme.

c Slant or half-rhymes are similar but not identical, e.g. *or mourn/some sunfull woman you/might have known.* Find one example of half-rhyme at the ends of lines in 'On Receiving a Jamaican Postcard'.

5 There are other sound patterns that produce echoes within and between lines. Answer the questions below to find out more about some of them.

a Alliteration is the repetition of consonant sounds at the beginning of words, e.g. *dancing at de edge of de sea.* Find two more examples of alliteration in 'On Receiving a Jamaican Postcard'. Suggest why the poet uses this.

b Consonance is the repetition of consonant sounds within words. It can be combined with alliteration, e.g.

Forest just stretch and stir.

consonance alliteration

Here it creates a hushed and gentle feel to reflect the sense of waking up. Copy the following lines and highlight the 's' sounds. Suggest why the poet uses this.

Forest dreaming of the caress of gold
Forest rootsing with the mysterious eldorado

c Assonance is the repetition of vowel sounds, e.g. *teeming creeping.* Read the line *Forest could keep secrets* aloud several times. Identify the two examples of assonance in it and suggest a reason for this use.

Check your learning

Copy out this verse from 'On Receiving a Jamaican Postcard', leaving plenty of room around it for annotations. Read it aloud several times. Highlight and annotate unusual word uses, evidence of Caribbean dialect and interesting features of rhyme and sound.

She a vision of frilly red
back-backing to he riddum
exposing she brown leg
arcing like lil mo
she will limbo into de sea

Compare your annotations with a partner's, adding anything you have missed out.

Learning extra

Grace Nichols makes much use of repetition in these poems. Identify how she uses repetition in two of them and comment on its effect.

Ted Hughes was Poet Laureate in the UK from 1984 until his death in 1998. He spent much of his early life in the Yorkshire countryside and his fascination with the natural world is clear in many of his poems.

Thistles

TED HUGHES

Your learning

Poets sometimes take something ordinary and use it to represent, or symbolise, something else. Here you will use annotation to investigate how Hughes presents thistles and uses them to symbolise other things.

Thistles

Against the rubber tongues of cows and the hoeing hands of men
Thistles spike the summer air
Or crackle open under a blue-black pressure.

5 Every one a revengeful burst
Of resurrection, a grasped fistful
Of splintered weapons and Icelandic frost thrust up

From the underground stain of a decayed Viking.
They are like pale hair and the gutturals of dialects.
10 Every one manages a plume of blood.

Then they grow grey, like men.
Mown down, it is a feud. Their sons appear,
Stiff with weapons, fighting back over the same ground.

EXPLANATIONS

hoeing a hoe is a tool for loosening soil

resurrection the dead being brought back to life

gutturals of dialects the throaty, harsh sounds of dialects (regional languages)

a plume of blood the plume is the feathery part of the thistle; it aids dispersal of the seeds. Here the dispersal of seeds is compared with the gushing of blood

feud a long-standing quarrel

1 Annotating a poem – making notes on words or ideas that stand out – can help you to develop your understanding of it. The example below shows annotations of the first stanza:

The first word suggests conflict and opposition

Against the rubber tongues of cows and the hoeing
hands of men
Thistles spike the summer air
Or crackle open under a blue-black pressure.

The gentle summer air is under attack; ***spike*** *suggests vicious and dangerous weapons*

Sense of danger and electricity with ***crackle*** *and* ***blue-black pressure,*** *which suggest a thunderstorm*

Copy the second and third stanzas onto the centre of a page. With a partner, write four annotations on interesting ideas or use of words.

2 Share your annotations with another pair. Add anything useful you had not thought of and delete anything you have changed your mind about.

3 Use the annotations on all three stanzas to help you find evidence to support each of the statements below.

- The thistles are engaged in a battle.
- Hughes creates a sense of time and history to show how long the thistles have been involved in this fight.
- The thistles are trying to reproduce and are fighting for survival.
- The thistles are presented as an aggressive force.
- They are compared to the Vikings, a race noted for their bravery.

4 A direct comparison of one thing to another, using 'like' or 'as', is a simile. In line 9 Hughes uses a simile to compare the thistles to humans. Explain how he develops this simile in lines 11–12.

5 Below are three opinions about the poem. Number them 1–3, where 1 is the one you most agree with. Use evidence from the poem to explain your choice.

- The thistles represent or symbolise strength and resistance.
- The thistles symbolise humans' constant fight for survival.
- The thistles are a symbol of the pointlessness of war.

Check your learning

We see symbols all the time. A dove, for example, is widely recognised as a symbol of peace. In groups of two or three, list as many symbols as you can and say what they represent. If possible, combine your ideas with those of other groups to make a class collection of widely recognised symbols.

Learning extra

Using what you learnt about patterns of sound on pages 92–3, identify and list examples of alliteration, consonance and assonance in 'Thistles'.

The Harvest Moon

TED HUGHES

Your learning

Poets often use figurative language. This may be metaphor, simile or personification. Here you will see how Hughes uses these three figures of speech.

The Harvest Moon

The flame-red moon, the harvest moon,
Rolls along the hills, gently bouncing,
A vast balloon,
Till it takes off, and sinks upward
5 To lie in the bottom of the sky, like a gold doubloon.

The harvest moon has come,
Booming softly through heaven, like a bassoon.
And earth replies all night, like a deep drum.

So people can't sleep,
10 So they go out where elms and oak trees keep
A kneeling vigil, in a religious hush.
The harvest moon has come!

And all the moonlit cows and all the sheep
Stare up at her petrified, while she swells
15 Filling heaven, as if red hot, and sailing
Closer and closer like the end of the world.

Till the gold fields of stiff wheat
Cry 'We are ripe, reap us!' and the rivers
Sweat from the melting hills.

EXPLANATIONS

harvest moon the full moon in September

doubloon a Spanish coin from many years ago

bassoon a woodwind instrument with a very low tone

vigil a watch that is kept, often at night

1 When someone says 'he flew out the door', they don't mean it literally. They are using the word 'flew' figuratively to show how quickly he went.

Writing about something as if it were something else is called metaphor. In the first stanza, Hughes refers to the moon as *a vast balloon* – think of the kind of balloon that is filled with gas and carries people.

a How does this metaphor help to capture the movement and appearance of the moon?

b How is this image of a vast balloon used again in the third stanza?

2 A direct comparison of one thing to another, using 'like' or 'as', is a simile. The first simile in the poem is of the moon lying in the sky *like a gold doubloon.* This conveys the colour of the moon, and also suggests that it is highly valued: just as a doubloon is a valuable foreign coin, so this moon is rare and exotic.

a Identify and copy the two other similes in the first stanza.

b What does each simile suggest?

c What is suggested by placing the two similes together?

3 Personification is where something that isn't human, such as an animal or an object, is described as though it were.

a **i** How is personification used in the second stanza to describe the trees?

ii What impression does it give of:

- the atmosphere that night
- the way the harvest moon is regarded?

There are two examples of personification in the final stanza.

b Identify and copy the first. What does it suggest about the wheat?

c Identify and copy the second. What does it suggest?

4 Poets use figurative language to create a picture and atmosphere for the reader. Re-read the poem and answer the question below, referring to the poem in your answer.

What impression are you given of the moon and its effects on people and nature?

Check your learning

Create a metaphor, a simile and an example of personification to describe each of the following:

- sunset
- an oak tree
- a dark street
- night
- an owl
- a star.

Compare your images with a partner's. Decide which ones are the most effective.

Learning extra

Either using the images you created in the 'Check your learning' activity, or using new ones, write the opening stanzas of a poem about night.

The Thought-Fox

TED HUGHES

Your learning

In this poem Hughes uses an extended metaphor of a fox to help the reader understand what it is like to write a poem. Here you will investigate this use of an extended metaphor.

The Thought-Fox

I imagine this midnight moment's forest:
Something else is alive
Beside the clock's loneliness
And this blank page where my fingers move.

5 Through the window I see no star:
Something more near
Though deeper within darkness
Is entering the loneliness:

Cold, delicately as the dark snow
10 A fox's nose touches twig, leaf;
Two eyes serve a movement, that now
And again now, and now, and now

Sets neat prints into the snow
Between trees, and warily a lame
15 Shadow lags by stump and in hollow
Of a body that is bold to come

Across clearings, an eye,
A widening deepening greenness,
Brilliantly, concentratedly,
20 Coming about its own business

Till, with a sudden sharp hot stink of fox
It enters the dark hole of the head.
The window is starless still; the clock ticks,
The page is printed.

EXPLANATIONS

clearings areas in woodland with few or no trees or shrubs

1 Put the statements below into the order in which they happen in the poem.

- **a** A fox emerges gradually, first his nose and then his eyes.
- **b** The fox is now brilliant and concentrated.
- **c** Something is approaching.
- **d** The poet, on his own late at night, is aware that something else is alive.
- **e** The fox boldly crosses the clearing.
- **f** The page is printed.
- **g** The page in front of the poet is blank.
- **h** The fox moves warily to the edge of the forest.
- **i** The fox enters the dark hole of the head.

2 A metaphor allows the poet to appear to be writing about one thing while actually writing about something quite different. In this poem, the emergence of a fox on a dark night represents the act of writing a poem.

Match each explanation below to the appropriate quotation to help you understand how Hughes develops this extended metaphor.

Explanation	Quotation
1 The poet has no ideas for the poem	a A fox's nose touches twig, leaf; Two eyes serve a movement
2 He has the first hint of an idea	b Of a body that is bold to come Across clearings, an eye, A widening deepening greenness
3 Only a small part of the idea is clear	c Till, with sudden sharp hot stink of fox It enters the dark hole of the head
4 The idea starts to take shape	d Something more near Though deeper within darkness Is entering the loneliness
5 His mind is freed to allow the idea to develop	e The page is printed
6 The idea takes possession of him	f Through the window I see no star
7 The poem is written	g Sets neat prints into the snow Between trees

3 Once we understand the metaphor of the fox, we are able to explore other images in the poem. What do the following things represent?

- the darkness
- the clearing
- the forest

Check your learning

Compare your answers to questions 1–3 with a partner's. Where there are differences, look back at the poem and decide whose answer is correct and why.

Learning extra

What has this poem told you about how it felt for Hughes to write a poem?

Linking the Ted Hughes poems

Your learning

Here you will be looking again at the three Ted Hughes poems on pages 94–8. You will explore the use of words, the linking of lines and stanzas and your personal response to the poems. You will be thinking, talking and writing about two or three poems together.

1 When we read poetry, we respond to both the sound of the words and the images they produce. Take, for example, the opening lines of 'Thistles':

> *Against the rubber tongues of cows and the hoeing hands of men*
> *Thistles spike the summer air*

The soft sound of *the rubber tongues*, *hoeing hands* and *summer air* is contrasted with the thistles' harsh *spike*. This gives a sense of their strength and determination. It also conveys the thistles' appearance and their action.

a Look through the poems. Find and copy two examples of language use that you find particularly effective.

b Describe the examples you have chosen to a partner and explain the reasons for your choice.

2 Each of the three poems reflects the poet's interest in the natural world.

a Using the poems as evidence for your ideas, mind-map features of Hughes's attitude to the natural world and its inhabitants, for example:

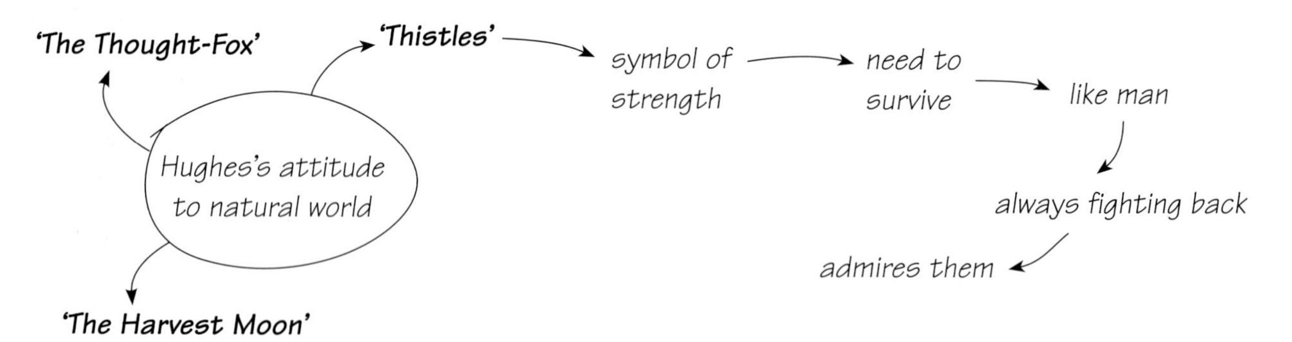

b In a small group, compare your mind-maps. Decide which one is the most useful and why.

3 Lines of poetry that have a clear pause at the end are called end-stopped lines. There are three in the following stanza:

> *So people can't sleep,*
> *So they go out where elms and oak trees keep*
> *A kneeling vigil, in a religious hush.*
> *The harvest moon has come!*

Sometimes one line of poetry runs on to the next with almost no pause. These are called run-on lines. They give an effect of continuity called enjambement.

a There is one run-on line in the stanza at the bottom of page 100. Which one is it?

b With a partner, read 'The Thought-Fox' aloud, paying close attention to the punctuation and the use of run-on lines. Hughes uses run-on lines at the end of three stanzas. Identify these and suggest why he uses them.

4 How much you like a poem depends on you and the effect the poem has on you. Often you may know which poems you like but find it difficult to explain why. In your explanation you should refer to what the poem made you think about, how it made you feel and which details (to do with content or language) affected you most.

a In a small group, talk about the poems you liked most and the ones you liked least. Question other members of your group closely on the reasons for their choices.

b Write a personal response to each of the three poems by Ted Hughes. You could use the sentence prompts below to help you.

The poem '...' made me think about ...
It made me feel ...
I liked/didn't like the way the poet ... because ...
An interesting example of language use is ...
I chose this because ...

Learning extra

Some people believe that Ted Hughes was the greatest English poet of the twentieth century. You will find many of his poems in anthologies and on the Internet. Read at least five more poems by Ted Hughes; choose the one you like most and prepare a two-minute talk on it, explaining why it appeals to you.

Check your learning

Look back on all the work you have done on the Hughes poems. Copy the table below and complete the boxes.

Features	Thistles	The Harvest Moon	The Thought-Fox
Evidence of symbolism			
Examples of metaphor and/or simile			
Examples of personification			
The theme of nature			
Examples of run-on lines			

Throughout human history, war has played its part. From the distant past to the present, there has never been a time when it did not exist. Countless lives have been lost to it and vast amounts of money continue to be spent on it. Is now the time to ask why?

Suicide in the Trenches

Siegfried Sassoon

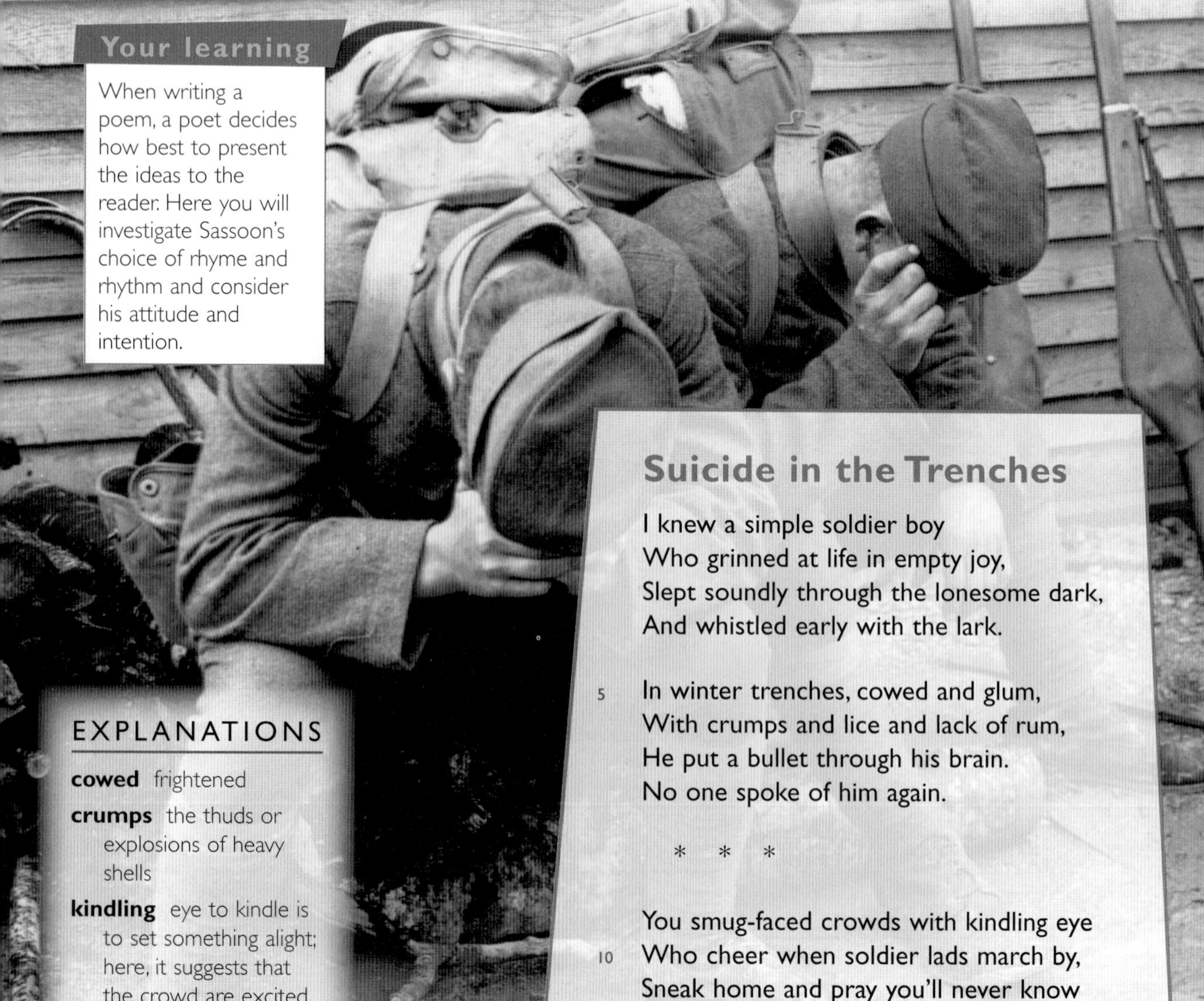

Your learning

When writing a poem, a poet decides how best to present the ideas to the reader. Here you will investigate Sassoon's choice of rhyme and rhythm and consider his attitude and intention.

Suicide in the Trenches

I knew a simple soldier boy
Who grinned at life in empty joy,
Slept soundly through the lonesome dark,
And whistled early with the lark.

5 In winter trenches, cowed and glum,
With crumps and lice and lack of rum,
He put a bullet through his brain.
No one spoke of him again.

* * *

You smug-faced crowds with kindling eye
10 Who cheer when soldier lads march by,
Sneak home and pray you'll never know
The hell where youth and laughter go.

EXPLANATIONS

cowed frightened

crumps the thuds or explosions of heavy shells

kindling eye to kindle is to set something alight; here, it suggests that the crowd are excited and enthusiastic

World War 1 (1914–18) was fought between the central powers (Germany, Austria–Hungary, Bulgaria and Turkey), and the allied powers (Britain and Empire, France, Belgium, Russia, Italy, USA). When it was over, up to 10 million men had died on the battlefield and 20 million were wounded.

1. The poem is written in three four-line stanzas (quatrains). Identify and write down what each quatrain is about.

2. Look back at page 84 to remind yourself about rhyme schemes.
   a. Identify the rhyme scheme in 'Suicide in the Trenches'.
   b. Look at the words Sassoon uses to rhyme. Suggest two reasons why Sassoon chose this rhyme scheme and these words.

3. Rhythms are all around us: ticking clocks, raindrops, heartbeats. Rhythm is essential to poetry; as in music, we look for the beat. The beat comes from a pattern of stressed and unstressed syllables. The symbols used to identify these are:

   ˈ used to indicate a strong or stressed syllable
   ˘ used to identify a weak or unstressed syllable
   For example:

   ˘ ˈ ˘ ˈ ˘ ˈ ˘ ˈ ˘ ˈ ˘ ˈ ˘ ˈ ˘ ˈ
   I knew a simple soldier boy// Who grinned at life in empty joy,

   a. Copy lines 3–4 from the poem and mark the strong and weak syllables. Read the lines aloud to help you.
   b. Find the line where the regular rhythm is broken. Suggest reasons for this.

4. Sassoon uses a simple rhyme scheme and simple vocabulary, perhaps to reflect the boy's simplicity, or to hide the seriousness of what he was writing about. To identify his real attitude and intention, answer the following:
   - Look at the first stanza. What is the boy like? Is he prepared for war?
   - Look at the second stanza. Why do you think the boy committed suicide?
   - Look at the third stanza. How would you describe its tone?
   - In your own words, explain the point Sassoon is making in the final stanza.

Check your learning

Here is the first stanza from another war poem by Sassoon, 'Does it Matter?'

Does it matter – losing your legs?...
For people will always be kind,
And you need not show that you mind
When the others come in after hunting
To gobble their muffins and eggs.

a. Identify the rhyme scheme.
b. Copy and mark the strong and weak syllables.
c. What is the tone of these lines? Give reasons for your answer.

Learning extra

Choose a serious subject that you feel strongly about. Present your ideas using a simple rhyme scheme and regular rhythm. You could use 'Suicide in the Trenches' as a model.

Green Beret

Ho Thien

Your learning

A narrative poem is one that tells a story. Here you will investigate the techniques Ho Thien uses to tell a story and his use of emotive language.

Green Beret

He was twelve years old,
and I do not know his name.
The mercenaries took him and his father,
whose name I do not know,
5 One morning upon the High Plateau.
Green Beret looked down on the frail boy
with the eyes of a hurt animal and thought,
a good fright will make him talk.
He commanded, and the father was taken away
10 behind the forest's green wall.
'Right kid tell us where they are,
tell us where or your father – dead.'
With eyes now bright and filled with terror
the slight boy said nothing.
15 'You've got one minute kid,' said Green Beret,
'tell us where or we kill father'
and thrust his wrist-watch against a face all eyes,
the second-hand turning, jerking on its way.
'OK boy ten seconds to tell us where they are.'
20 In the last instant the silver hand shattered the
sky and the forest of trees.
'Kill the old guy' roared Green Beret
and shots hammered out
behind the forest's green wall
25 and sky and trees and soldiers stood,
in silence, and the boy cried out.
Green Beret stood
in silence, as the boy crouched down
and shook with tears,
30 as children do when their father dies.
'Christ,' said one mercenary to Green Beret,
'he didn't know a damn thing
we killed the old guy for nothing.'
So they all went away,
35 Green Beret and his mercenaries.

And the boy knew everything.
He knew everything about them, the caves,
the trails the hidden places and the names,
and in the moment that he cried out,
40 in that same instant,
protected by frail tears
far stronger than any wall of steel,
they passed everywhere
like tigers
45 across the High Plateau.

EXPLANATIONS

Green Beret the headwear of the American Special Forces

mercenary a hired soldier fighting for financial gain

In 1961 the USA became involved in the war in Vietnam. Failure to defeat the guerrilla forces and opposition at home led to a US withdrawal in 1973. The USA had suffered 200,000 casualties, with 58,000 killed or missing.

1. A narrative is a story. This story is told in chronological order, which is the order in which things happened. Write a list showing the order of events in the poem. The first two are done for you.
   - *Mercenaries capture boy and father.*
   - *Green Beret decides to frighten boy to make him talk.*

2. The narrator is the persona or voice the poet adopts to tell the story.
   a Read the following statements about the narrator. List the ones you think are true, and write down supporting evidence from the poem.
   The narrator is:
   - not directly involved in the story
   - someone who sees and hears everything
   - the boy looking back on his own past
   - on the side of the boy
   - a journalist
   - a mercenary.

   b Write a paragraph describing the role of the narrator in this poem. Refer to the poem to support what you say.

3. Dialogue adds realism to the story. What does it show you about:
   - Green Beret
   - the mercenary.

4. Writers sometimes use words to appeal to readers' emotions and influence their response. This is called emotive use of language. Read the lines below and the comment on them.

Green Beret looked down on the frail boy//with the eyes of a hurt animal	*The fact that Green Beret 'looked down' on the boy emphasises that the boy is small. The boy is referred to as 'frail', suggesting he is weak and easily broken. He has the eyes of a 'hurt animal', suggesting helplessness. These words help to make the reader feel sorry for the boy.*

   Find and copy two other references to the boy where the language is emotive. Explain how the poet has chosen words to appeal to the reader's emotions.

5. The second stanza concludes the story. What does it reveal about:
   - the boy
   - the people Green Beret and his mercenaries are fighting?

Check your learning

The way a narrative poem tells a story can influence a reader's response. Use what you have learnt about this poem to help you decide whose side the writer wants the reader to take. Give at least four clear reasons, based on the poem, for your answer.

Learning extra

Use your library and the Internet to research the Vietnam War and find out more about the role of the Green Berets and the Vietnamese resistance.

The Sorrow of Sarajevo

GORAN SIMIĆ

Your learning

It is not always necessary to describe something in great detail. Here you will examine the technique of *understatement* and consider the use of repetition and the word *association*.

The Sorrow of Sarajevo

The Sarajevo wind
leafs through newspapers
that are glued by blood to the street;
I pass with a loaf of bread under my arm.

5 The river carries the corpse of a woman.
As I run across the bridge
with my canisters of water,
I notice her wristwatch, still in place.

Someone lobs a child's shoe
10 into the furnace. Family photographs spill
from the back of a garbage truck;
they carry inscriptions:
Love from … love from … love …

There's no way of describing these things,
15 not really. Each night I wake
and stand by the window to watch my neighbour
who stands by the window to watch the dark.

The siege of Sarajevo (5 April 1992 to 29 February 1996) was the longest siege in modern history. It was fought between the forces of the Bosnian government and Serbian paramilitaries. An estimated 12,000 people were killed and another 50,000 wounded during the siege.

1 The poet focuses on the ordinary, everyday things of life, such as a newspaper. What other ordinary, everyday things are referred to?

2 Sometimes, by focusing on a few well chosen details and presenting them simply, the poet can tell the reader a great deal. In this poem, it is the poet's references to ordinary things that convey the horror of war.

a What does he tell us about each of the following: the newspapers, the wristwatch, the child's shoe, the family photographs?

b In what ways are these things unexpected?

c How do the details about everyday things convey the horror of war?

3 Sometimes a poet can achieve a particular effect through understatement. (This means saying less about something rather than more.)

a What examples can you find of common features of poetry such as adjectives, similes, metaphors? Why might the poet have used so few?

b What does line 14 suggest to you?

4 Certain words make us think of other things and create a broader image, for example:

*The Sarajevo wind//**leafs** through newspapers*

The word *leaf* has different associations. It could suggest:

- a page in a book or newspaper
- the action of turning pages
- a leaf blowing in the wind.

Consider the highlighted words below. What do you associate with them? What do they suggest to you?

- newspapers//that are glued by blood to the street
- Someone lobs a child's shoe
- Family photographs spill//from the back of a garbage truck.

5 **a** Identify the two lines in the poem where repetition is used.

b Why do you think repetition is used in each of these places?

Check your learning

a Explain what is meant by 'understatement'.

b Sarajevo was devastated by bombing. Explain how this is shown to the reader through:

- the details
- the language.

Learning extra

Imagine a conversation between the speaker in the poem and his/her neighbour. Use details from the poem and information about the siege of Sarajevo to write the dialogue for their conversation.

Linking the *Words of war* poems

Your learning

Here you will look again at the three poems on pages 102–6. You will also read a piece of writing about them on page 109, considering how it has been structured and identifying some of its features for comparison.

1. When you start to write about more than one poem, you need to gather ideas. Below is part of a mind-map for comparing the poems. Think of more points to add to it.

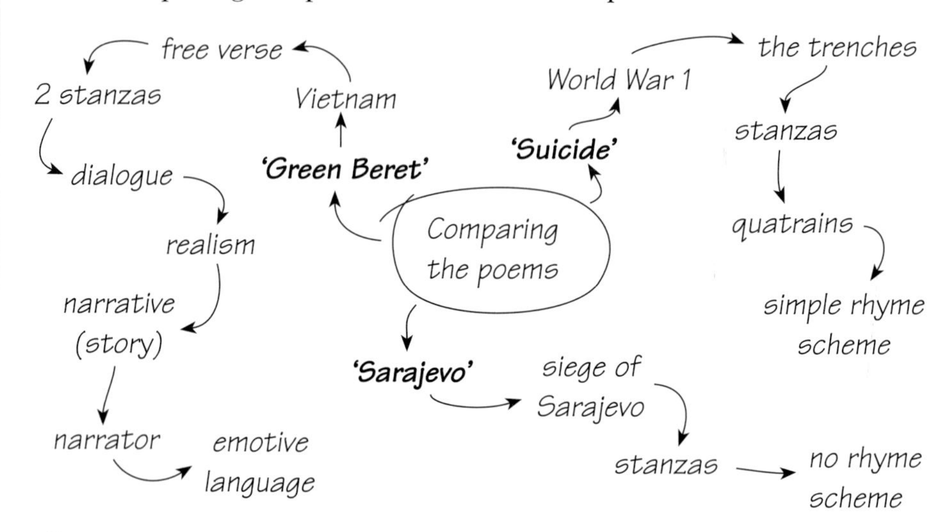

2. You now need a clear outline of what you are going to cover in each paragraph. The critical comparison on page 109 is organised into four paragraphs:

   Paragraph 1: the different settings of the three poems
   Paragraph 2: the different structures of the three poems
   Paragraph 3: the use of language in 'Green Beret' and 'Suicide'
   Paragraph 4: the use of language in 'Sarajevo'

   Read the comparison on page 109 and identify, from the mind-map, the points that went into each paragraph.

3. The writer uses words and phrases such as 'also' and 'in contrast' to point out similarities and differences between the poems. Write down all the words and phrases used to make connections between the poems.

4. How often does the writer quote directly from the poems? List the quotations used.

5. The writer has developed comments, making suggestions about the poems' meanings and why the poets wrote as they did. The comments in the first two paragraphs are highlighted for you. Identify and copy the comments in paragraphs 3 and 4; you should find at least five.

These three poems are about three quite different wars and highlight different aspects of those wars. 'Green Beret' refers to the Vietnam War and relates an incident in which a young boy is threatened with the death of his father. The poet seems to suggest that the brutal action of the soldiers only makes the resistance stronger. 'Suicide in the Trenches', on the other hand, is about World War I and focuses on the life and death of one 'simple' soldier boy. It shows how desperate life in the trenches was, and challenges the popular view on war. 'The Sorrow of Sarajevo' deals with yet another war – the siege of Sarajevo. It shows the effects of the war on the everyday lives of the people who lived there.

The poets adopt different methods to present their ideas. In 'Green Beret', Thien uses a narrative approach. He relates the incident as though it were a story, describing, in order, the things that were said and done. This poem is written in free verse. The first long stanza describes what happened and the shorter second stanza focuses on the resistance forces and how they have not been defeated. In contrast 'Suicide in the Trenches' is written in three quatrains, with a simple rhyme scheme and regular rhythm. Sassoon might have used this form to emphasise the simplicity of the boy who killed himself. 'The Sorrow of Sarajevo' is also written in four-line stanzas, though there is no rhyme scheme and the rhythm is irregular.

The poets use language differently. Thien uses dialogue, possibly to give a sense of realism and to show exactly how Green Beret spoke. We see how heartless he is when he commands 'Kill the old guy' in front of the son. He also uses language emotively and describes the boy as having 'the eyes of a hurt animal'. This makes the reader feel sympathy for the boy and take the boy's side against Green Beret. Sassoon uses fairly simple vocabulary in his poem, with few adjectives and no similes or metaphors. There is a harsh brutality in the directness of the lines:
'He put a bullet through his brain.
No one spoke of him again.'
This perhaps is to reflect the harsh reality of war.
Simić also uses fairly simple vocabulary with no imagery, perhaps to support his statement that 'There's no way to describe these things'. Unlike Sassoon and Thien, Simić chooses everyday things to write about, such as newspapers, a wristwatch and family photographs. He links them, however, with unusual things. The newspapers are 'glued by blood to the street'. The wristwatch is on the wrist of a corpse and the family photographs 'spill' from a garbage truck. By placing these ordinary things in extraordinary contexts, the writer manages to convey the devastating effects of the war on the lives of ordinary people.

Learning extra

Write a further paragraph comparing the three poems. Write about the poem you liked most; say why you preferred it and why you did not choose the other two.

Check your learning

Compare your answers to questions 1–5 with a partner's. Discuss the reasons for any differences.

Reading one poem often leads us to make links with other poems we have read. There may be similarities in subject matter, theme or style. In this section, you will consider two pairs of poems and explore the links between them.

Tramp

RUPERT M. LOYDELL

Your learning

These two poems have different cultural backgrounds: one is English and the other Indian, but they deal with similar subjects. Here you are going to explore their similarities and differences. You will also revise your learning on how to refer to, and comment on, a poem.

Tramp

This mad prophet
gibbers mid-traffic,
wringing his hands
whilst mouthing at heaven.

5 No messages for us.
His conversation is simply
a passage through time.
He points and calls.

Our uneven stares dissuade
10 approach. We fear him, his
matted hair, patched coat,
grey look from sleeping out.

We mutter amongst ourselves
and hope he keeps away. No
15 place for him in our heaven,
there it's clean, and empty.

EXPLANATIONS

prophet a person who predicts future events, often associated with religion

gibbers talks rapidly and unintelligibly

wringing clasping hands together in despair

Poverty Poems – 2

NISSIM EZEKIEL

Poverty Poems – 2

I lifted up my eyes
near the railway station
and saw a leper standing
against a poster-ridden wall.

Silent, a beggar, (5)
he did not beg.
Offered a coin
he took it
without a glance at me
nor made the slightest gesture (10)
in acknowledgement. Perhaps
he was dumb and deaf as well.

Dumb and deaf
I walk along
leper-image sinking in my eyes. (15)
There was another on the platform:
he sang with zest in praise of God
like a happy saint
which perhaps he was…
I walk along, (20)
leper-music holding up my mind.

EXPLANATIONS

leper a person suffering from leprosy, a disease that can cause severe deformities

zest enjoyment and energy

When comparing poems it is useful to have a framework. A table like the one below allows you to look at different aspects of the poems together.

a Copy the table and, with a partner, make notes on the areas to investigate.

Areas to investigate	Tramp	Poverty Poems – 2
The meanings Make notes on: • how the people in the poems are described • what they say or do • how the speaker responds to the people • the endings of the poems		
Interesting features Make notes on: • the ways the ideas are organised in the poem • the use of language – give examples and comment on them		
The poets' attitudes Make notes on: • what the poets' attitudes appear to be • the poems' 'messages'		

b Either highlight similarities between the poems in one colour and differences in a different colour, or list similarities under one heading and differences under another.

Page 83 shows you how to refer to a poem to support the points you make about it. Look back at that page, or at the notes you made, to remind yourself how to do this.

a Copy and complete the following statements, using appropriate quotations from the box on the left. Remember to use inverted commas when quoting.

- In the first verse of 'Tramp' the speaker refers to the tramp as being a _______ whereas in the first verse of 'Poverty Poem – 2' the speaker calls the man _______.
- The tramp in the first poem is _______ but the beggar in the second poem is _______.
- Both the tramp and the beggar ignore the speakers. The tramp has _______ and the beggar takes the coin _______.
- The speaker in 'Tramp' is afraid of the tramp and says: _________. The speaker in 'Poverty Poems – 2' feels that he, like the beggar, is _______ until he meets a second beggar.

> no messages for us
> mad prophet
> mouthing at heaven
> silent
> We mutter amongst ourselves/ and hope he keeps away
> without a glance at me
> a leper
> dumb and deaf

b Compare your answers with a partner's. Make sure they have put inverted commas around their quotations.

c Write two more statements about the two poems; use quotations in both of them.

3 Look back at page 83 to remind yourself how to develop your comment. Useful phrases to introduce comments are:

- 'This suggests ...'
- The poet seems to be saying ...'
- 'This shows the reader ...'
- 'The way the poet describes the tramp makes me think that ...'

Choose two of the statements in question 2 and develop a comment for each one.

5 Good responses to poetry show the reader using their own ideas to explore, investigate and interpret meaning. Useful phrases that help you to explore a poem's meaning or a poet's intentions are:

- 'This could suggest ...'
- 'One way of interpreting this is ...'
- The poet might be implying that ...'
- 'Perhaps the poet wants to ...'

Below is an example of exploration and interpretation.

No
place for him in our heaven,
there it's clean, and empty.

The poet includes the reader in this statement by using 'our'. He seems to suggest that the people who fear and keep their distance from the tramp fail to see him as equal in the eyes of God: 'No place for him in our heaven'. They forget, however, that no one is completely 'clean'. By failing to help him, or at least trying to help, the poet implies that they too are not 'clean' or suited for heaven. The heaven they imagine is 'empty'.

Choose two extracts from the poems. For each one, use your own ideas to explore and interpret meaning.

Check your learning

Write 8–10 sentences comparing what both poets seem to be saying about tramps and beggars. Make sure you:

- ✪ develop your comments
- ✪ use quotations to support the points you make.

Learning extra

Using information from the poems and your own knowledge, write a newspaper article on street beggars in which you:

- describe the situation
- give your personal views.

Swinging

Gillian Clarke

Your learning

Both of these poems deal with the relationship between a parent and a child. Here you will investigate and compare how each poet reveals this relationship and write a response on this. You will use your speaking and listening skills to help you prepare for the writing.

Swinging

At the end of the hot day it rains

Softly, stirring the smells from the raked
Soil. In her sundress and shorts she rocks
On the swing, watching the rain run down
5 Her brown arms, hands folded warm between
Small thighs, watching her white daps darken
And soak in the cut and sodden grass.

She used to fling her anguish into
My arms, staining my solitude with
10 Her salt and grimy griefs. Older now
She runs, her violence prevailing
Against silence and the Avenue's
Complacency, I her hatred's object.

Her dress, the washed green of deck chairs, sun
15 Bleached and chalk-sea rinsed, colours the drops,
And her hair a flag, half and then full
Mast in the apple-trees, flies in the face
Of the rain. Raised now her hands grip tight
The iron rods, her legs thrusting the tide
20 Of rain aside until, parallel
With the sky, she triumphs and gently
Falls. A green kite. I wind in the string.

EXPLANATIONS

daps plimsolls or trainers

prevailing winning, overcoming

complacency smugness and self-satisfaction

Nettles

VERNON SCANNELL

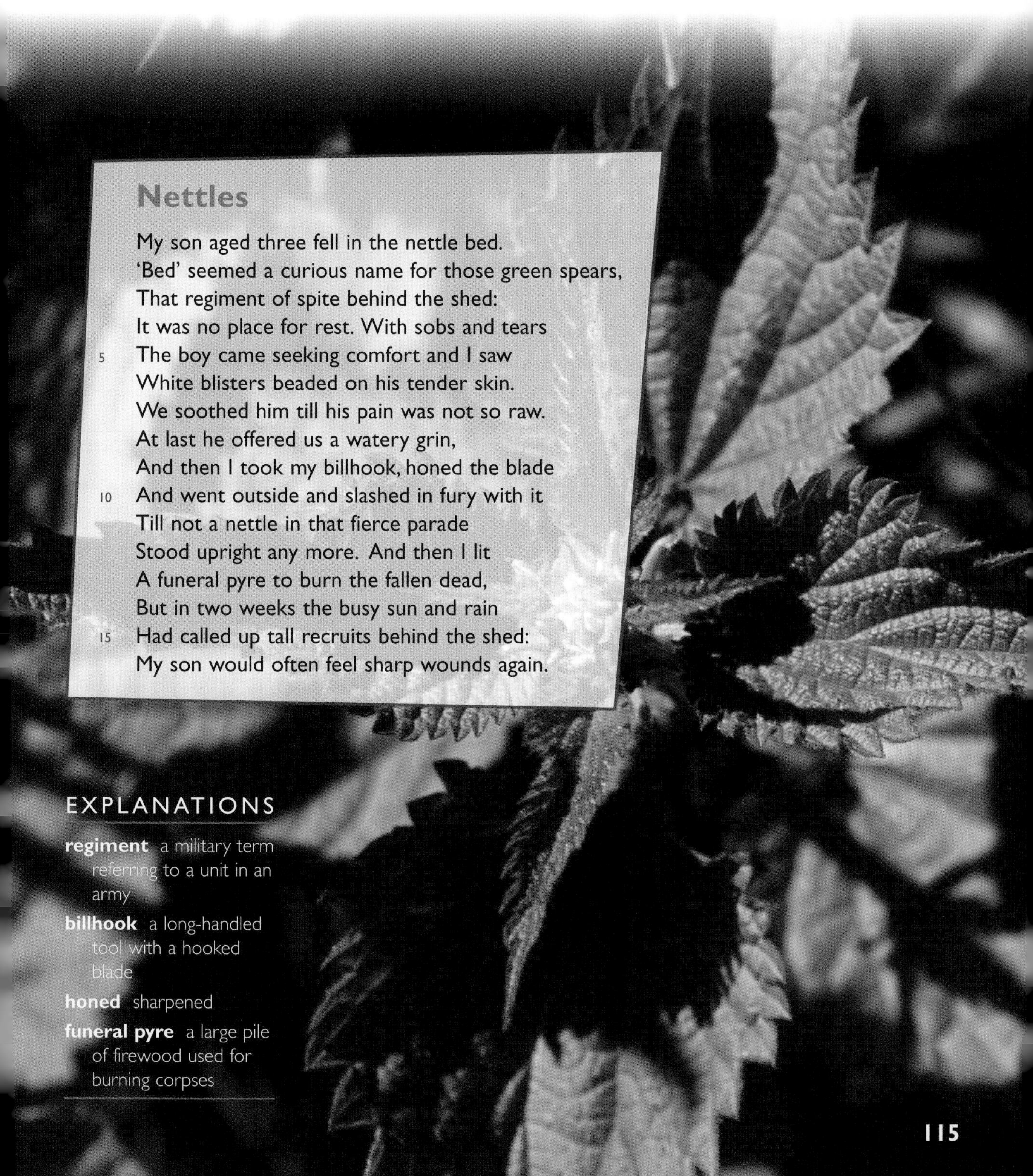

Nettles

My son aged three fell in the nettle bed.
'Bed' seemed a curious name for those green spears,
That regiment of spite behind the shed:
It was no place for rest. With sobs and tears
5 The boy came seeking comfort and I saw
White blisters beaded on his tender skin.
We soothed him till his pain was not so raw.
At last he offered us a watery grin,
And then I took my billhook, honed the blade
10 And went outside and slashed in fury with it
Till not a nettle in that fierce parade
Stood upright any more. And then I lit
A funeral pyre to burn the fallen dead,
But in two weeks the busy sun and rain
15 Had called up tall recruits behind the shed:
My son would often feel sharp wounds again.

EXPLANATIONS

regiment a military term referring to a unit in an army

billhook a long-handled tool with a hooked blade

honed sharpened

funeral pyre a large pile of firewood used for burning corpses

1 When studying poetry it helps to share ideas with others. Listening to other people's views helps us to see things we might not otherwise have seen.

In a group of four, read each poem aloud, then pool your ideas on it. Nominate one person to record the group's ideas on a large sheet of paper to share with the class later. Some prompts are listed below to help you get started.

Swinging

- *What happens?*
- *How is the poem structured?*
- *In what different ways is the daughter described?*
- *How does the writer show the energy and defiance of the child?*
- *How is the movement of the swing captured in the girl's movement?*
- *Find and comment on interesting uses of the sounds of words.*
- *What is suggested by the last line?*
- *What are you shown about the relationship between mother and daughter?*

Nettles

- *What happens?*
- *What imagery is used for the nettles?*
- *How is the son described?*
- *What are the father's feelings?*
- *What happens to the nettles?*
- *What might the last line mean?*
- *What might the nettles symbolise?*
- *What are you shown about the relationship between father and son?*

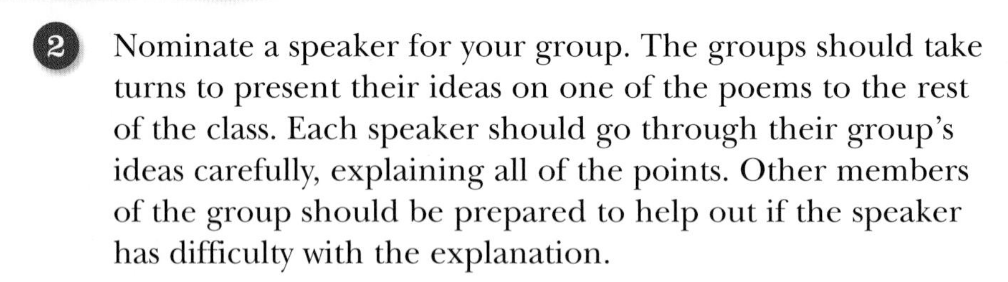

2 Nominate a speaker for your group. The groups should take turns to present their ideas on one of the poems to the rest of the class. Each speaker should go through their group's ideas carefully, explaining all of the points. Other members of the group should be prepared to help out if the speaker has difficulty with the explanation.

Listen carefully to all the presentations and make separate notes on things that are said that you had not thought of. Afterwards, the groups' notes can be pinned around the classroom as reminders.

3 Divide your group into two pairs.

a Each pair should work together to list points that could be made in answer to the following:

Compare the ways a parent–child relationship is shown in 'Nettles' with the way it is shown in 'Swinging'.

b Compare your list with the other pair's list. Add to your list any points you did not have that you agree with.

c Compare your list with another pair from a different group. Add to your list any points you did not have that you agree with. Your list should now contain the ideas of six people.

4 You are now ready to start organising the ideas to help you write an answer to the task in question 3a. Remember to refer to the poems to support the things you say and to develop your comments. Below is a suggested structure to help you with your writing.

Introduction: explain briefly that both poems deal with a parent's relationship with a child. State briefly what these relationships are, i.e. father/young son; mother/growing and changing daughter.

Section 1: use your notes to help you write about 'Nettles', explaining what you learn about the relationship and the methods Vernon Scannell uses to show you this.

Section 2: use your notes to help you write about 'Swinging', explaining what you learn about the relationship and the methods Gillian Clarke uses to show you this. Refer back to 'Nettles' to highlight similarities and differences between the poems.

Conclusion: summarise the main similarities and differences between the poems. Say which poem you liked most and give reasons for your preference.

Check your learning

Swap your answer with a partner's. Assess their work against the criteria below. For each criterion award 1, 2 or 3 marks, where 3 = most effective.

a Have they explained the relationship in 'Nettles' clearly?
b Have they explained the relationship in 'Swinging' clearly?
c Have they written about the methods Vernon Scannell uses?
d Have they written about the methods Gillian Clarke uses?
e Have they referred to the texts to support the things they say?
f Have they developed their comments?
g Have they pointed out similarities and differences between the poems?

At the end, write a comment using these criteria to help you point out the things your partner has done well and the things they need to improve on.

When you get your answer back, read your partner's comments carefully.

Learning extra

Studying poetry closely helps us to read the next poem we choose with greater understanding of technique and appreciation of meaning. Make poetry part of your regular reading. It only takes a few minutes to read a good poem and, sometimes, the ideas in them will stay with you throughout your life.

Interactive Poetry 11–14 skills and Framework Objectives

The following chart outlines the main reading/writing (*) skills and where particular Framework Objectives can be addressed.

	Student Book skills	Software skills	Student Book F/W Os	Software F/W Os
Section A				
Norman Silver				
Electronic Brain	Personification Repetition Voice/ persona	Structure Word choice	R7, R8	W14, R14, R19
I Want Trainers	Narrator/ poet Simile	Themed language Alliteration	R9, R16	W14, R14
Life is a Ball	Metaphor Extended metaphor Personal response	Understanding Theme	R14	W14, R14
Linking the poems	Personal response	Understanding	R6, R12	R19
John Agard				
The Soldiers Came	Structure Stanzas Message	Structure Simile, metaphor, personification Alliteration, assonance	R7, R12, R19	R6, R7, R14
What The Teacher Said …	Using quotations* Cultural context	Themed language Rhyme	R7, R8, R14, R19	R9, S16
Checking Out Me History	Social/ historical context Message Using quotations*	Social/historical context Accent and dialect	R7, R8, R14, R19	R9, S16
Linking the poems	Personal response Comparing	Word choice Themes	R19	R6
Elizabeth Jennings				
The Moth's Plea	Alliteration Personification	Verbs Imagery Theme	R8, R12	R14, W17
Casting a Spell	Extended metaphor Writing a poem*	Rhyme Structure Themed language	Wr9	W14, R14
The Fish's Warning	Pauses Word choice	Ideas in the poem Figurative language	R12, R14	R8, R14
Linking the poems	Comparing Personal response	Understanding	R17	W14
Theme: Playing with words				
Why English is so Hard	Rhyme Writing a poem*	Rhyme Structure Plurals	R14, Wr8, Wr9	S2, W14, R19

Little Acorns	Poetic devices Poetic forms Assonance	Assonance Poetic devices Poetic forms	W9, R14, Wr9	W21, R19
Facing the truth – with Haikus	Form Characterisation	Form Structure Characterisation	R12	R9, R19
Linking the poems	Alliteration Rhythm Syllables Writing a poem*	Understanding	Wr8, Wr9	R7
Poem pairing				
Jabberwocky and Jabbermockery	Parody Word choice Onomatopoeia	Parody Themed language Structure	W16, R6, R14, R19	R7, R19
Section B				
Benjamin Zephaniah				
Wot a pair	Humour Personification	Humour Non-standard English	R4	S11, R7
According to my mood	Attitude Non-standard English	Non-standard English Author's craft	Wr8, Wr9	S8, W12, W13
Important notice	Imperatives Repetition	Message Imperatives	R10	R5, R7, R16
Linking the poems	Personal response Considering the poet	Understanding	R4	R5, R16
Jackie Kay				
English Cousin comes to Scotland	Dialect Repetition	Dialect Standard English Understanding	S12, R7, R16	S11, R16
Tomorrow they'll be coming to get me	Voice/ persona	Punctuation Author's craft Narrative	R4, R10	R5, R7
Pollution	Personification Structure	Verbs and adjectives Reading of the poem	R5, R10	W8, R5
Linking the poems	Titles Structure Message	Understanding	R7, R13, R16	R13
William Blake				
The Tyger	Alliteration Repetition Rhyme Theme	Understanding Alliteration	R15	R5, R11
Holy Thursday (Experience)	Rhetorical questions Contrasts Message	Rhyme Structure Images	R10	R16
London	Repetition Imagery Social/ historical context	Word choice Social/ historical context Imagery	R10	R11, R15

Linking the poems	Social/ historical context Comparing	Word choice Understanding	R13, R15	W11, R13
Theme: Through my eyes				
Weekend visit	Emotions Form Personal response	1st and 2nd person Informal language	R11	S12, R16
Grandfather	Descriptive language Characterisation	Themed language Alliteration	R10	W11, R10
Quieter Than Snow	Simile Atmosphere Appealing to senses	Atmosphere Similes and metaphors	R10	W11, R7
Linking the poems	Comparing Form 1st person Writing a poem* Drafting*	Understanding	Wr1, Wr9	R7, R11
Poem pairing				
The Boy with a Cloud in his Hand and **He Wishes for the Cloths of Heaven**	Descriptive language Endings	Adjectives Understanding	R10	W11, R7
Poem pairing				
Shakespeare's Sonnet 18 and **Shakespeare's 18th Worm**	Form Parody Metaphor Comparing Writing a comparison*	Rhyme Word choice Structure Personification	R5, R14, Wr18	W11, R14
Section C				
Thomas Hardy				
A Light Snow-Fall after Frost	Word choice Simile Oxymoron	Rhyme Structure Adjectives	W6, W7	W7
Heredity	Theme Exploring an idea	Rhyme Structure Word choice	W7, R11	W7, R11
The Walk	Writing a detailed answer*	Word choice Understanding	W7, R5, Wr3, Wr17	R11, R12
Linking the poems	Language over time Social/ historical context Rhyme Considering the poet Personal response	Word choice Understanding	S11, R5, R15	W7, R11, R15
Grace Nichols				
On Receiving a Jamaican Postcard	Tone Repetition Cultural context	Dialect Cultural context	R16, R11, R12	S10, W7, R16

Two Old Black Men on a Leicester Square Park Bench	Free verse Structure	Structure Figurative language	R6, R16	W7, R11
For Forest	Imagery	Rhyme Assonance Repetition Personification	W7, R11, R12	W7
Linking the poems	Cultural context Non-standard English Word choice Rhyme Sound patterns	Understanding	S10, W7, R5, R12, R16	R6, R7, R16
Ted Hughes				
Thistles	Annotating a poem* Simile Symbolism	Word choice Alliteration	W7, R12, Wr1	W7, R11
The Harvest Moon	Figurative language: metaphor, simile, personification	Structure Oxymoron Figurative language	W6, W7, R12	W7
The Thought-Fox	Extended metaphor	Rhyme Assonance Understanding	W6, W7	W7, R12
Linking the poems	Sounds Attitude Pauses Personal response	Word choice	W7, R7, R11, R12	W7, R6, R7
Theme: Words of war				
Suicide in the Trenches	Social/ historical context Rhyme and rhythm Quatrains Attitude	Rhyme Structure Word choice Images	W7, R11	W7, R6, R11
Green Beret	Social/ historical context Narrative technique Emotive language Attitude	Structure: narrative Nouns, verbs, adjectives Repetition Metaphor	R6, R7, R11	W7, R6, R16
The Sorrow of Sarajevo	Social/ historical context Understatement Word choice	Word choice Verbs	W7, R7, R11, R12	R7, R11, R16
Linking the poems	Planning a written response* Organising and writing a comparison*	Understanding	R6, R7, R16, R17, Wr3	R7, R16
Poem pairing				
Tramp and **Poverty Poems – 2**	Comparing Using quotations* Writing a comparison* Personal response	Characterisation Comparing Understanding ideas	R6, R7, R17, Wr3, Wr17	W7, R7, R16
Poem pairing				
Nettles and **Swinging**	Speaking and listening Writing a comparison*	Word choice Understanding ideas Comparing	R7, R17, Wr3, S&L7, S&L10	W7, R7

Glossary

alliteration

where two or more words that are close together start with the same sound, as in 'Quieter Than Snow':

At every desk a still child stared at me
Teachers walked through walls and back again

assonance

where a poet places similar-sounding vowels together, as in 'Little Acorns':

if the hickory's trick is the limerick

caesura

a definite pause in the middle of a line, usually marked by a full stop, as in 'The Fish's Warning':

stare
At my quick gliding, my darting body. You're made of air
And I of water.

cinquain

a poem of twenty-two **syllables**, in five lines of two, four, six, eight and two syllables

consonance

the repetition of consonant sounds within words, as in 'Quieter Than Snow':

No racks of bikes
No kicking legs, no fights,

couplet

a pair of lines that go together, either because they **rhyme** (a rhyming couplet), or because they form a separate **stanza** on their own. This couplet, from 'Shakespeare's 18th Worm', both rhymes and is a stanza in its own right:

So long as worms can squirm or hedgehogs fast,
So long as birds are late your life will last.

dactylic metre

a rhythm created by stressing the first of every two syllables, as in 'Important notice':

Silence glows and makes no sound
some will try to keep you down.

dialogue

a conversation between two people, for example 'Facing the truth – with Haikus'

enjambement

an effect of continuity created by running one line into the next without a break, as in 'Casting a Spell':

Rich in subtle rhythms and
Right words which most will understand.

figurative language

language that poets use to create a picture and atmosphere for the reader, usually in the form of **metaphor**, **simile** or **personification**. Yeats uses figurative language in 'He Wishes for the Cloths of Heaven', when he says:

I have spread my dreams under your feet;
Tread softly because you tread on my dreams.

free verse
lines of poetry that do not fit a fixed rhythmic pattern, but can be of any length the poet chooses. Lines in free verse tend to follow the meaning and/or the natural rhythm of the words, as in 'English Cousin comes to Scotland':

> I got skelped because I screamed when a skelf
> went into my pinky finger: OUCH, loud.
> And ma ma dropped her best bit of china.

haiku
a poem with three lines and 17 **syllables**. The first and third lines have five syllables each, and the second line has seven, as in 'Facing the truth – with Haikus':

> A mere three lines long
> Just seventeen syllables
> Simple, pimple – right?

Haikus were first written in Japan, to describe Nature

iambic metre
a rhythm created by stressing the second of every two syllables, as in 'Jabberwocky':

> One, two! One, two! And through and through
> The vorpal blade went snicker-snack!

imagery
descriptive language that creates a picture in the reader's mind; it often takes the form of **metaphor**, **simile** or **personification**. 'For Forest' contains several examples of imagery, such as *darkness wrap her like a gown.*

limerick
a five-line poem, usually humorous, with a distinctive rhythm and the **rhyme scheme** a-a-b-b-a. The English writer Edward Lear wrote many famous examples, including:

> There was an Old Man with a beard,
> Who said,'It is just as I feared! –
> Two Owls and a Hen,
> Four Larks and a Wren,
> Have all built their nests in my beard!'

lyric
a poem, usually quite short, that expresses the poet's feelings and emotions about something, as in 'Casting a Spell':

> Casting a spell's a secret skill
> Which few learn fast. No act of will
> On your part hands the gift to you.

metaphor
where a poet describes one thing as if it is something else, as in 'Pollution':

> The anger in her eyes is a brilliant torch.

Sometimes a poet sustains this technique throughout a poem, as in 'Life is a Ball', where the speaker describes his/her life to being kicked around like a football. When a poet does this, it is called an extended metaphor

metre
another name for **rhythm**

monologue
a piece spoken by one person, as in 'English Cousin comes to Scotland'

narrative
a poem that relates the events of a story in chronological order, as in 'Green Beret'

onomatopoeia
where the name of a thing or an action sounds like the thing or action itself, for example *snicker-snack* and *chortled* in 'Jabberwocky'

oxymoron
where two words that apparently contradict one another are placed together, for example *dark snow* in 'The Thought-Fox', and *the silence / Rolled like thunder* in 'Quieter Than Snow'

parody
a comic imitation that creates humour by exaggerating the features of the piece it imitates. 'Jabbermockery' is a parody of 'Jabberwocky' (even its title says so!); it uses a similar rhyme scheme, follows Lewis Carroll's storyline closely, and adapts the words to form new ones, such as *Miss Borogrove* and *slickersmack*

personification
giving human characteristics to something that is not human, like the poet's runaway trousers in 'Wot a pair':

> De pair addressed me rather blunt,
> And they told me they were sick of being put on
> Back to front.

pun
a play on words where one word is used to mean two things, for example in 'I Want Trainers', where in the line *that stamp your identity on the streets*, the word *stamp* means both the stamping of feet and the assertion of the speaker's identity

quatrain
a four-line stanza, usually following a regular **rhyme scheme**, as in 'Holy Thursday' and 'Suicide in the Trenches'. In both these examples, the poets have chosen a simple structure to convey a serious message

rhyme
the repetition of a sound from word to word or from one line to another. When rhyme occurs at the close of lines it is called end rhyme. Internal rhyme is the repetition of a sound within or between the lines of a poem, as in 'Grandfather': *Patterned to a latticework of lines*. Half-rhymes (or slant rhymes) are repeated sounds that are similar but not identical, as in this stanza from 'Shakespeare's 18th Worm':

> Sometime too wet the mouth of heaven spits,
> And often are the segments clogged with **dirt**,
> And every squirm from squirm sometime desists,
> By chance of nature's sending in a **bird**.

rhyme scheme
the pattern of end rhyme in a poem. Lines with the same end rhyme are given the same letters, so for example in 'Electronic Brain', the first stanza has the rhyme scheme a-a-b-b-a

rhythm
(also called metre) the pattern of stressed and unstressed syllables in a poet's choice of words. Rhythm can be regular, as in **dactylic** and **iambic metre**, or irregular, as in **free verse**. A poet can change the rhythm of a poem to achieve striking effects, as in 'Suicide in the Trenches', where the last line of the second stanza (*No one spoke of him again*), breaks the regular rhythm of the rest of the poem

shape poem
a poem whose words and/or lines make a shape or pattern on the page, for example:

if the apple counts in syllables
if the firs prefer free verse
if the plum makes puns
THEN
LET
THIS

simile
a comparison using 'as' or 'like', as in 'Quieter Than Snow': *silence hung in the yard like sheets* and *the first September leaves / Dropping like paper*

sonnet
a poem with fourteen lines and the **rhyme scheme** a-b-a-b, c-d-c-d, e-f-e-f, g-g. The **rhythm** is also fixed – see Shakespeare's 18th Sonnet on page 74, which is a typical example

stanza
(also called a verse) a group of lines that make up a distinct unit in a poem, similar to a paragraph in prose. Not all poems are divided into stanzas, and a stanza can be of any length, so 'Thistles' is written in four stanzas of three lines each, while 'Grandfather' has one stanza of sixteen lines, followed by one of ten, then one of four

syllable
a single sound within a word, so for example, 'poetry' has three syllables: po + et + ry

symbolism
where a poet uses one thing to stand for something else, as in 'The Thought-Fox', where the appearance of a fox represents the gradual process of writing a poem

tanka
a poem of thirty-one **syllables**, in five lines of five, seven, five, seven and seven syllables. Tankas were first written in Japan where they were used to describe and 'round off' all kinds of events and occasions

tone
the writer's voice; it may be humorous, angry, cheerful, serious, ironic or any number of feelings. The tone of a poem may change as the poem progresses, as in 'Nettles', where the poet's tone moves from sympathy for his hurt child, to anger at the nettles, to accepting the fact that he cannot protect his son from everything in life

villanelle
a **lyric** poem of nineteen lines in three-line stanzas and ending with a **quatrain**. The first and third lines of the first stanza are repeated throughout the poem

Heinemann is an imprint of Pearson Education Limited, a company incorporated in England and Wales, having its registered office at Edinburgh Gate, Harlow, Essex, CM20 2JE.
Registered company number: 872828

Heinemann is a registered trademark of Pearson Education Limited

First published 2006

11
10 9 8 7

British Library Cataloguing in Publication Data is available
from the British Library on request.

ISBN 978 0 435761 81 3

Designed by Lorraine Inglis
Produced by Kamae Design
Printed in China (CTPS/07)
Cover photo: © Getty Images
Illustrations on pages 36–7 by Andy Morris

Acknowledgements
The author and publisher would like to thank the following individuals and organisations for permission to reproduce photographs:

p13 Corbis/Bettman, Corbis/Kim Kullish, p14 Alamy/David Crausby, Getty/Stephen Stickler; p15 Rex Features, Alamy/Steve Atkins p17 Corbis/Otto Rogge, Empics; p18 Corbis/Harcourt Index, SPL/Lawrence Lawry; p19 Topfoto p21 Harcourt Index, Corbis/Darrell Gulin; p22 Topfoto; p23 Oxford Scientific, Alamy/Nick Kirk; p25 Corbis/Jack Novak, Getty; p26 Harcourt Index, Harcourt Index; p27 Alamy/Brian Mitchell, Alamy/Peter Bowater; 29 Topfoto, Popperfoto; p39 Corbis/Trapper Frank; p40 Alamy/Peet Simard, Rex Features/Dean Pictures; p41 Corbis/Mathew McKee, Getty Images/Christopher Bissell; p43 Corbis/WildCountry, Rex Features; p44 Corbis/Gavriel Jecan, Corbis/Frans Lanting; p45 Getty Images/Paul Edmondson, Profimedia.CZ s.r.o/Alamy; p47 Alamy/Marc Hill, Bridgeman Art Library/William Blake; p48 Topfoto, Bridgeman Art Library/William Blake; p49 Corbis/Hulton-Deutsch, Bridgeman Art Library/William Blake; p51 Corbis/Carols Barria, Photolibary.com/Richard Bloom; p52 Getty Images/Christopher Furlong, Alamy/Darren Matthews; p53 Rex Features/Nigel Barklie, Alamy/John Rensten; p55 Getty Images/Photodisc, Oxford Scientific/Richard Packwood; p56 Corbis/Kim Sayer, Rex Features/Richard Austin; p66 Getty Images/Jan Tove Johansson, Getty Images/Derek Redfearn; p67 Getty Images/Hans Neleman, Corbis/Simon Marcus; p68 Corbis/Bettman, Gloucestershire, 1890, Topfoto; p70 Corbis, Lonely Planet/Greg Johnston; p71 Corbis/Kevin Fleming, Rex Features/Jeremy Sutton Hibbert; p72 Louie Psihoyos/Corbis, Anup Shah/Nature PL; p74 Alamy/David Boag, Rex Features/A Searle; p75 Alamy/Photolibrary Wales, Corbis/Paul Hardy; p76 Getty Images/Paul Nicklen, Alamy/Niall Edwards; p78 Corbis/Hulton-Deutsch, Corbis; p79 Topfoto/Mark Godfrey, Corbis/Bettman; p80 Alamy/Network photographers, Corbis/maps.com; p82 Alamy/Homer Sykes, Getty Images/Philippe Coste; p83 Getty Images/Adrian Weinbrecht, Topfoto.

Every effort has been made to contact copyright holders of material reproduced in this book. Any omissions will be rectified in subsequent printings if notice is given to the publishers.

'Checking Out Me History' by John Agard. Copyright © 1996 by John Agard, reproduced by kind permission of John Agard c/o Caroline Sheldon Literary Agency. 'The Soldiers Came' by John Agard. Copyright © 1990 by John Agard, reproduced by permission of John Agard c/o Caroline Sheldon Literary Agency. 'What The Teacher Said When Asked: What Er We Avin For Geography, Miss?' by John Agard. Copyright © 1996 by John Agard, reproduced by permission of John Agard c/o Caroline Sheldon Literary Agency Limited. 'Life Is A Ball', 'I Want Trainers' and 'Electronic Brain' by Norman Silver. Copyright © Norman Silver. Reprinted with the kind permission of the author. 'The Moth's Plea', 'Casting a Spell' and 'The Fish's Warning' by Elizabeth Jennings, from *A Spell Of Words* published by Macmillan. Reprinted with permission of David Higham Associates Limited. 'Little Acorns' by David Horner, slightly adapted, from *So There!* Published by Apple Pie Publications in 1993. Copyright © David Horner 1993. Reprinted with the kind permission of the author. 'Facing the Truth – with Haikus' by Malorie Blackman from *Cloud Busting*, first published by Corgi Yearling. © Oneta Malorie Blackman 2004. Reproduced by permission of The Agency (London) Ltd, all rights reserved and enquires to The Agency (London) Ltd 24 Pottery Lane, London W11 4LZ fax 0207 727 907 and also permission of The Random House Group Ltd. 'Jabbermockery' by Trevor Millum. Copyright © Trevor Millum. Reprinted with the kind permission of the author. 'Wot a pair' by Benjamin Zephaniah, Copyright © Benjamin Zephaniah. Reprinted with the kind permission of the author. 'According to my mood' by Benjamin Zephaniah from *Talking Turkeys* by Benjamin Zephaniah (Viking 1994) Copyright © Benjamin Zephaniah 1994. Reprinted with permission Penguin Books UK. 'Important notice' by Benjamin Zephaniah, from *The Dread Affair* published by Arena Books. Copyright © Benjamin Zephaniah. Reprinted with the kind permission of the author. 'English Cousin comes To Scotland', 'Tomorrow they'll be coming to get me' and 'Pollution' by Jackie Kay from *Two's Company* published by Puffin. © Jackie Kay. Reprinted with the kind permission of the author. 'Quieter Than Snow' by Berlie Doherty, from *Walking On Air* published by HarperCollins.© Berlie Doherty Reprinted by permission of David Higham Associates Ltd. '*Weekend Visit*' by Alan Smith, from *Tapestry* edited by Michelle Williams. Copyright © 2004 John Wiley & Sons Australia www.jaconline.com.au. 'Grandfather' by Susan Hryknow. 'Shakespeare's 18th Worm' by Celia Warren first published in *The Unidentified Frying Omelette* Andrew Fusek Peters, published by Hodder Children's Books, 2000 © Celia Warren 2000. Reprinted with the kind permission of the author. 'The Boy With A Cloud in His Hand' by Sheenagh Pugh, from *The Beautiful Lie*, published by Seren Books in 2002. Reprinted by permission of Seren Books. 'He Wishes For The Cloths of Heaven' by W.B. Yeats. Reprinted with permission of A P Watt Ltd on behalf of Michael B. Yeats. 'On Receiving a Jamaican Postcard' by Grace Nichols from *Lazy Thoughts Of A Lazy Woman* by Grace Nichols. Copyright © Grace Nichols 1989. Reproduced by permission of Curtis Brown Group Ltd on behalf of Grace Nichols. 'Two Old Black Men on a Leicester Square Park Bench' by Grace Nichols from The Fat Black Women's Poems by Grace Nichols, Copyright © Grace Nichols 1994. Reproduced with permission of Curtis Brown Group Ltd on behalf of Grace Nichols. 'For Forest' by Grace Nichols, from *Come On Into My Tropical Garden* by Grace Nicols. Copyright © Grace Nichols 1988. Reproduced with permission of Curtis Brown Group Ltd on behalf of Grace Nichols. 'The Thought-Fox', 'Thistles' and 'The Harvest Moon' by Ted Hughes, from *New Selected Poems 1957–1994* published by Faber and Faber. 'The Sorrow of Sarajevo' by Goran Simić, (English version by David Harsent) © David Harsent 1997. Reprinted with the kind permission of David Harsent. 'Green Beret' by Ho Thien, from *Axed Between the Ears* by David Kitchen, published by Heinemann. 'Suicide in the Trenches' by Siegfried Sassoon, from *Collected Poems 1908–1956* published by Faber and Faber. copyright © Siegfried Sassoon by kind permission of Mr George Sassoon c/o Barbara Levy Literary Agency. 'Tramp' by Rupert Loydell. Copyright © Rupert Loydell. Reprinted with the kind permission of the author. 'Poverty Poems – 2' by Nissim Ezekiel, from *Poverty Poems*. Reprinted by permission of Oxford University Press India, New Delhi. 'Nettles' by Vernon Scannell, from *New And Collected Poems* Robson Books Ltd 1950. Copyright © Vernon Scannell. Reprinted with the kind permission of the author. 'Swinging' by Gillian Clarke, from *Collected Poems* published by Carcanet Press Ltd. Reprinted with permission of Carcanet Press Ltd

p48 The Times Educational Supplement, *Poetryclass*; p86 The Poetry Society www.poetrysociety.org.uk.